WITHDRAWN

Dolph Briscoe Center for American History
THE UNIVERSITY OF TEXAS AT AUSTIN

JFK'S FINAL
HOURS IN TEXAS

An Eyewitness Remembers
the Tragedy and Its Aftermath

JULIAN READ

Ebook available from RosettaBooks (www.rosettabooks.com)

Requests for permission to reproduce material from this work should be sent to Office of the Director, Dolph Briscoe Center for American History, The University of Texas at Austin, 2300 Red River Stop D1100, Austin, TX 78712-1426.

∞ The paper used in this book meets the minimum requirements of ANSI/NISO z39.48-1992 (R1997) (Permanence of Paper).

Library of Congress Control Number: 2013949048

Photo, previous pages: *President and Mrs. Kennedy's joyous arrival at Love Field in Dallas.*

CONTENTS

FOREWORD

I know Julian Read as a fixture in the world of Texas politics and public affairs and also as a passionate advocate for historical preservation. He's been a stalwart supporter of the Briscoe Center, and I'm proud to say his papers are part of our holdings. I was aware of his close relationship to Governor John Connally and knew of Julian's proximity to the historic events surrounding John F. Kennedy's final trip to Texas. There are plenty of Texans with their own stories to tell of that November in Dallas, but few with this sort of inside seat to the crisis. So, when Julian approached me to share his memoir, I was immediately intrigued.

Reading Julian's recollections evoked my own vivid memories of JFK's final hours in Texas. Like many of my generation, Kennedy was the first candidate who inspired my political awareness. At the age of thirteen, I handed out his campaign's bumper stickers and leaflets at shopping centers in my hometown, Dallas, and skipped school to watch the inauguration on television.

On that fateful day in 1963, the Dallas school district had granted permission for students to leave school to see the president downtown or at Love Field, but I was stranded at home with car trouble. I heard about the assassination while eating lunch and ended up watching Walter Cronkite's news coverage. (I would later have the good fortune to call Walter a close friend, and we spoke at length about the death of JFK while working on Cronkite's memoirs.) As a resident of Dallas, there were even more personal connections—friends and their families were the local police and politicians involved in the aftermath. The infamous photo of Jack Ruby shooting Lee Harvey Oswald is notable to me as a historian, but also as a collection of familiar faces from my neighborhood. Those moments were brought back to me as I read Julian's retelling of that tragic time.

This memoir would have value if Julian had simply recounted his own experiences during Kennedy's ill-fated trip to Texas. But he goes on to provide an important, and often overlooked, aspect of the assassination. What does it mean to be the site of such a tragedy? How does a community negotiate that complex legacy? Julian explores how the public memory of those events has been shaped, from monuments and museums to the annual remembrances of those directly involved. His extensive research and interviews with key figures, paired with his own insider's perspective, have resulted in a compelling book that gives a uniquely Texan perspective to a national tragedy.

Don Carleton
Executive Director, the Dolph Briscoe
Center for American History

JFK'S FINAL HOURS IN TEXAS

Texas Governor John Connally with aides, left to right: Mike Myers, Julian Read, Howard Rose, Connally, Larry Temple, and John Mobley.

INTRODUCTION

On Friday, November 22, 1963, one of the most shocking and tumultuous events in history occurred shortly after noon when the president of the United States, John Fitzgerald Kennedy, was struck down by an assassin's bullet in downtown Dallas, Texas.

It is difficult for today's generation to fully comprehend the trauma that gripped the nation and the world for days and weeks afterward.

Grown men sobbed shamelessly in public.

Streets were deserted.

Schools and shops were shuttered.

Terrified mothers lowered window shades.

Businesses came to a standstill.

Churches and synagogues were crowded as never before.

Americans were fearful and uncertain as they remained glued to television screens, watching a nightmare that would defy any screenwriter's imagination unfold before their eyes.

As a nation, we watched a usually stolid Walter Cronkite brush away a tear as he announced on the CBS television news that the president was dead. With our neighbors we mourned the sight of the president's body being unloaded from Air Force One at Andrews Air Force Base outside Washington, D.C., while the new president, Lyndon Baines Johnson, stood on the tarmac facing the task of calming an uneasy nation against mounting rumors of conspiracies. Then, less than forty-eight hours later, we were horrified and dumbfounded to see, on live television, the murder of the president's accused assassin in—of all places—the basement of the Dallas police headquarters. What more could happen?

It all seemed too much for our generation to endure, and the scars of those events did in fact remain for a long, long time.

I was a witness to that momentous tragedy fifty years ago as an aide to Texas Governor John B. Connally, who was the host for the five-city tour that brought the president to Texas, and ultimately to Dallas. I was Connally's representative to an army of news editors and reporters who covered the widely anticipated tour of Texas, the state that had given the Kennedy-Johnson ticket the winning edge in the election of 1960.

Then, for years following the assassination, each and every November I scheduled and coordinated a seemingly endless progression of interviews for Governor Connally with representatives of news media from around the world who repeatedly revived the tragedy on its anniversary date. After Governor Connally's death in 1993, I continued to coordinate the same requests that persisted for his wife, Nellie Connally, until she died in 2006.

But through these many years, I never have shared my

personal experiences of that horrendous time that will remain etched in the nation's memory and psyche. I now feel, at the fiftieth anniversary of the assassination, that my viewpoint, for whatever it is worth, should be added to the record.

I would ask the reader to be mindful that this is not a book about Julian Read. It's a book about incomprehensibly shattering events that Julian Read, then a thirty-six-year-old campaign consultant early in his career saw, heard—lived through—a half century ago in Dallas on November 22, 1963.

This is not a book about me, although I'm at the center of it and keep popping up in the most unlikely places throughout the account of events that I witnessed on that history-changing weekend and in its aftermath. Even now, as I probe my memory and the memories of those who lived through those days with me and are still able to share them, I find it something of a wonder: why was I even there in the first place?

I began what ultimately led to my career as an eighteen-year-old cub reporter for the venerable *Fort Worth Press*, a Scripps-Howard operation. I decided, at age twenty-four, to open my own public relations/advertising business. I experienced some ups and downs and held on long enough to get a chance to work with an upstart underdog politician named Jim Wright. The former mayor of Weatherford, Texas, had decided to challenge the choice of the Fort Worth power elite in a race against a three-term incumbent for his seat in the U.S. House of Representatives. Jim Wright won that race—against all odds, really—beginning a career of service in that office that spanned decades and ended up with him serving as Speaker of the House of Representatives. My service and counsel in that first campaign was something Speaker Wright never forgot and never failed to commend to others.

Well aware of that political victory and several that had preceded it, John Connally was contemplating his own uphill race to unseat the sitting governor of Texas, Price Daniel, in the upcoming 1962 Democratic primary. Connally, an acolyte of Lyndon Johnson during Johnson's ascent to power, looked for the same qualities in his team that Johnson had demanded of him—natural ability, a tireless work ethic, and unflagging loyalty. Connally sensed those qualities in me, and based on that and my record with Congressman Wright's campaign, he took me on to help guide his media effort.

It is difficult for younger generations to know, or older generations to remember, how primitive the advertising media were in those days, especially compared to today's world in which we are under a constant information assault from our publications, our mail, our televisions, our computers, and even our telephones. At the time I joined the fledgling Connally for Governor campaign, television, as a political medium, was in its infancy, far subordinated, for example, to billboard advertising.

Nonetheless, at my suggestion, the campaign produced and aired a series of filmed "morning visits," called *Coffee with Connally*, which featured Connally and members of his family at a breakfast table, with a steaming cup of coffee placed before the remarkably handsome candidate, as he gave a brief, seemingly offhand assessment of one of the leading issues of the campaign. It was a setting in which he was very comfortable—informal, somewhat rural in flavor (in keeping with his background, which still peeked through his evident sophistication), and to the point.

The public fell in love with John Connally. His poll

numbers went from a humbling 4 percent at the campaign's outset to a decisive primary victory over a field of five candidates, one of whom was the incumbent governor. That campaign was the beginning of my long relationship with John Connally that endured on many levels—and never with a written contract—until I helped to coordinate his funeral services after his death in 1993.

Whatever common ground we shared—both of us were sons of poor Texas dirt-farming families—John Connally and I moved through our careers and lives together for more than thirty years. I was intimately involved with him and his family in almost any important occasion of which they were a part; in effect, I was his consigliere.

It was in that role that I found myself on that iconic day in Dallas, although my official function was to help manage the press corps covering the Kennedy tour of Texas, which included the historic motorcade and the events that ensued. As events overtook us all, that assigned role quickly evaporated, and I found myself in uncharted territory, in far deeper waters than I ever could have imagined.

I was there, and this is my account of what my viewpoint revealed during those days of incredible tragedy, tension, and stress. Perhaps the most amazing aspect of it all is how close I came to watching the whole thing unfold on television from my office in Austin.

More important than my experiences during those seminal times, of course, is the history of what happened—and what did not happen—relating to that watershed event since then. I have been fortunate to watch those fifty years of history in the making from the perspective of a native Texan who was not only present for the body blows of that horrific day in Dallas but also over the weekend that followed and throughout the traumatic months—truly years—of recovery in the aftermath. Accordingly, I have devoted months of concentrated effort to explore and reconstruct milestones and sidelights of the long and often difficult journey from that time of mourning and anguish to a time of remembrance and reconciliation for Dallas, Texas, and the world.

I have done so to document not only the immediate agony endured by the people who found themselves in the epicenter of the tragedy but also the continuing human experience of individuals and a wounded community dealing with recovery from the pain that ensued year after year. The review of that five-decade journey is followed by my personal perspective on the legacies of the Kennedy assassination to our state and our nation.

CHAPTER ONE

||||||||||||||||||||||||||||||||||||||||||||||||||||||||||||||||||||||||||||||||||||||||||||||||||||||||||||||||||||||||||||||||||||||||||

THE DAY THAT TIME STOOD STILL

Virtually every living person old enough to remember can tell you precisely where he or she was on November 22, 1963, when the news broke that President John Fitzgerald Kennedy had been shot in Dallas.

And they will insist on telling you where they were and what they were doing without prompting.

It is a remarkable phenomenon—perhaps the most universally shared experience in our nation's history.

Where were you at that fateful moment? If you were not yet born, or too young to remember, you likely have heard the memories of your elders.

I was riding in the White House press bus that was part of the ill-fated JFK motorcade in downtown Dallas, within full view of President Kennedy's limousine, which was driving slowly less than 200 yards ahead, uncovered for the day to allow the public clear views of the first couple.

I was seated among one of the most distinguished collections of reporters ever assembled outside of Washington, D.C. It included such all-stars as Robert Pierpoint, CBS News; David Broder, *Washington Star*; Tom Wicker, *The New York Times*; and Peter Lisagor, *Chicago Daily News*. The list went on and on.

They all had come to the key state of Texas the morning before, interested in gauging support for the president's reelection the following year.

Furthermore, this was the first public appearance of First Lady Jacqueline Kennedy since the loss of their infant son, Patrick Bouvier Kennedy, a few months earlier, and there was much interest in her state of mind.

Earlier that morning in nearby Fort Worth, following an overnight stay there, the press had watched Kennedy thrill a huge crowd of partisan supporters at an outdoor rally in a misting rain and charm a packed audience of business leaders at a Chamber of Commerce breakfast. It had been a triumphant start to the day.

I then joined the reporters as they boarded the same Pan American charter that had brought them from Washington. We preceded the presidential entourage aboard Air Force One on a fourteen-minute flight to Dallas Love Field.

Now, barely thirty miles away from Fort Worth and less than an hour later, the press buses had picked us up at the airport, and we were rolling along Main Street in the heart of downtown Dallas, just a few vehicles behind the presidential limousine. Four of the reporters—Merriman Smith (UPI), Frank Cormier (AP), Bob Baskin (*Dallas Morning News*), and Bob Clark (ABC)—had moved up for their turns in the coveted "pool car" positioned immediately behind the president's vehicle.

For weeks in advance, there had been ominous clouds of hostility toward the president in Dallas, raising concerns for his safety in an open car. The city had experienced nasty, somewhat violent demonstrations previously against vice presidential candidate Lyndon B. Johnson several years earlier and against United Nations Ambassador Adlai Stevenson much more recently. Upon arriving in Dallas, President Kennedy was greeted by handbills accusing him of treason and a similar full-page attack advertisement framed with a black border in the *Dallas Morning News*.

However, at this moment, the mood inside the bus was anything but ominous.

The air was filled with light banter akin to a holiday outing. Reporters were uniformly surprised by the warm reception for the president and his wife. They saw a large cheering crowd meet the couple and their hosts, Governor Connally and Nellie Connally, at Love Field. In fact, the reception was so warm as to prompt President Kennedy to break away from Secret Service agents momentarily to shake hands being extended along the airport fence. The welcome continued. Throngs of well-wishers lined streets all the way to downtown. And now, amazingly, sidewalks were jammed along Main Street with ever-growing crowds. Overhead, hundreds hung out of the windows of office buildings.

Buoyed by the friendliness, the two beaming couples were kept busy waving their response to the rising chorus of cheers. It was becoming clear that the president and the first lady were warmly welcomed in Dallas.

Our press bus had turned right onto Houston Street and was in sight of a seven-floor red brick building, the Texas School Book Depository. In just a few moments, we would turn left and follow the limousine down Elm Street past that building. Then, exiting downtown, it would be on to the Dallas Trade Mart, where 2,400 luncheon attendees were buzzing in anticipation of their first glimpse of the handsome president and his glamorous first lady.

At this moment, there was no hint that a few heartbeats later, time would stand still.

CHAPTER TWO

||||||||||||||||||||||||||||||||||||||||||||||||||||||||||||||||||||||||||||||||||||||||||||||||||||||||||||||||||||||||||

WHY THE PRESIDENTIAL TRIP TO TEXAS?

In the opening chapter of William Manchester's book *The Death of a President*, the author laments that the president "had to go to Texas." He blames that necessity on the need to mend deep political differences in the state between liberal Senator Ralph Yarborough and the more conservative Lyndon Johnson–John Connally forces. The necessity for the Texas visit ostensibly was in the interest of boosting Kennedy's reelection chances the following year—1964.

Manchester goes on to suggest that the president felt that Vice President Johnson should have been able to handle this matter alone, and thus viewed the trip as an "imposition."

While every author is entitled to his view based on what he knows—or thinks he knows—what Manchester purports is not the way it was, even though Kennedy voices have succeeded in embedding that myth into the assassination narrative for decades.

In fact, the trip was about money—Texas money that Kennedy badly wanted.

There was no question that a wide and long-standing schism existed between Yarborough and Johnson, this despite the truth that, as Governor Connally and others have observed, both men were in Washington almost constantly, readily accessible to the president anytime he wanted to call them together to address the rift. However, the president made no such overture to either of the parties.

After all, regardless of their differences, Texas Democrats had united to carry the state for Kennedy in 1960 and indeed provided the crucial margin to enable him to become the president of the United States.

Certainly, if a visit to the state went well, it could be expected to strengthen the president politically. But the real reason that Kennedy had for some time been pressing both the vice president and Governor Connally to sponsor a trip to Texas was for fund-raising purposes. Those overtures had begun after Connally's election in the fall of 1962.

In his own book, *In History's Shadow*, Connally points out that as a new governor he had been preparing for his first legislative session and settling into office since his November election. He therefore had resisted planning such an involved and ambitious undertaking as a presidential trip. Moreover, there was another very practical reason for his hesitation. While Connally was personally fond of President Kennedy, having served as his Secretary of the Navy prior to his election as governor, he recognized that Kennedy was not all that popular in Texas and was unsure whether he might be able to marshal his own broad following to ensure success of a trip to the state.

But despite Connally's equivocation, the president was

persistent in his fascination with "rich Texans," continuing to push for the development of plans for a Texas fundraising trip.

Former Connally aide Larry Temple well remembers accompanying the governor to a meeting with the president and Vice President Johnson in El Paso in June 1963.

Connally told Temple immediately after that meeting that the president had once again vigorously advanced the idea of the trip and that this time, the governor and the vice president had acquiesced.

The White House envisioned a series of fund-raisers in major Texas cities, to which Connally objected, arguing, "You don't want to look like you just want to come down here and rape the state [of money]." He had a broader vision for the trip. As he told his wife, First Lady Nellie Connally, he was confident that Texans would come around to like Kennedy if exposed to him properly, in the right settings.

To bring this about, Connally would draw on his own political strength and influence with the Texas power structure to conceive an ambitious, largely nonpartisan plan.

That plan developed in this manner: The president, the first lady, and staff members would board Air Force One in Washington on the morning of Thursday, November 21, and depart for San Antonio. More than a dozen Texas members of Congress who did not want to miss the big event would accompany them on board.

A separate Pan American Airways charter press plane was to follow, carrying more than fifty members of the White House Press Corps. As noted, they were curious about how the president would be received three years after his election in the state that provided his winning margin. Their journalistic appetites also were whetted by the surprise announcement that the glamorous first lady would accompany the president, the result of a specific request by Governor Connally. It would be her first visit to Texas, so she was sure to hear a lot about the state's storied history, going back to its days as a republic, and hopefully she would be intrigued. Moreover, if all the plans failed to generate much excitement, Kennedy operatives stood ready to feed the Press Corps titillating inside information about the Johnson-Yarborough differences, just to spice things up.

The presidential party would be received in San Antonio by their hosts, Texas Governor John Connally and wife Nellie Connally from Austin, as well as Vice President Johnson and wife Lady Bird Johnson, who would fly in from the LBJ Ranch to join the welcoming party. Together, they would motor through San Antonio, stop to greet schoolchildren along the way, and help dedicate a new medical research facility at Brooks Air Force Base.

With the San Antonio events completed, the party would reboard their planes and fly to Houston to participate in a mammoth testimonial dinner that evening for stalwart Congressman Albert Thomas.

The long eventful day would end with a flight to Fort Worth's Carswell Air Force Base. From there, the presidential entourage would motorcade downtown, where the president and first lady would retire at the Hotel Texas to rest in preparation for an even busier day ahead.

Early Friday morning, a ballroom packed with a throng of leading Fort Worth citizens would await the first couple downstairs at a nonpartisan Chamber of Commerce breakfast. Before attending that event, however, the president would join Vice President Johnson, Senator Ralph Yarborough, Congressman Jim Wright, and state Senator Don

Kennard at a partisan rally of Democratic supporters in a parking lot across the street.

After breakfast, the presidential party and Press Corps would retrace the few miles back to Carswell, reboard their planes, and fly the fourteen minutes to nearby Love Field in Dallas. There, they would be greeted by local dignitaries and then would set off on a motorcade through downtown Dallas, finishing at the Dallas Trade Mart, a popular local exposition center. A select crowd of the city's most prominent citizens would gather there to see and listen to a president whom many of them never supported.

The luncheon was planned as a nonpartisan gathering cosponsored by the powerful conservative Dallas Citizens Council, the Dallas Assembly, and the Science Research Center. The blockbuster event would be a testament to the political muscle of Governor Connally.

Beyond the events of Dallas awaited Austin and the climactic evening in the state's capital, including the massive political fund-raiser that President Kennedy had craved for so long. To properly frame that centerpiece event, John and Nellie Connally would open the Governor's Mansion and residence that afternoon to present the president and first lady to members of the Texas Legislature and their spouses.

Finally, perhaps eighteen hours after the morning breakfast that began the day, Vice President Johnson and Lady Bird would welcome the president and first lady as overnight guests at their LBJ Ranch near Stonewall, sixty miles west of Austin. It would be Johnson's opportunity to host Kennedy on his own home soil for only the second time.

To make the most of the visit, they would entertain their guests on Saturday, offering the quintessential Hill Country experience—a traditional Texas barbecue lunch in front of the ranch house on the banks of the Pedernales River. How could they resist this longtime Johnson trademark?

That was the plan, grandly and intricately conceived and designed to meet the diverse objectives of all parties. Pulling it off was the challenge that lay before us.

CHAPTER THREE

||||||||||||||||||||||||||||||||||||||||||||||||||||||||||||||||||||||||||||||||||||||||||||||||||||||||||||||||||

BUMPS ALONG THE PLANNING WAY

I t was inevitable that differences would arise between respective parties as specific plans for the president's visit began to be addressed.

The Kennedy White House and the Democratic National Committee were interested primarily in raising money and in ensuring that Kennedy's supporters had ample opportunities to see the president. Once the trip was agreed to, their operatives, along with a legion of Secret Service agents, swarmed all across the state.

While Governor Connally had no quarrel with those objectives, he felt that the president, as well as Vice President Johnson, would benefit best from a mostly nonpartisan trip. In political terms, he valued the loyalists, but he wanted nonbelievers to be exposed to Kennedy so they could see that he did not have horns.

As is usually the case, the differences emerged in the details. And there were lots of cooks in the kitchen. So it quickly became evident that there was need for a strong, energetic voice to provide coordination between host Governor Connally and the myriad interests involved.

Enter the young Benjamin Frank Barnes, a rising star approaching the status of phenomenon on the Texas political scene in 1963. Elected to the Texas House of Representatives at age twenty-one from the hardscrabble hometown of De Leon in central-west Texas, Barnes was one of only three House members who had opposed sitting Governor Price Daniel and instead supported John Connally in his race for governor in November 1962. That was only one year before President John F. Kennedy's trip to Texas. Already a favorite in Connally circles, and with political savvy beyond his years, Barnes naturally would be involved in Connally-sponsored plans for the trip. With the added sponsorship of Frank Erwin, the powerful secretary of the State Democratic Executive Committee, and the blessing of Speaker of the Texas House Byron Tunnell, Barnes was designated to be a liaison between Connally forces and the Kennedy White House.

It was a role that Barnes relished and engaged in quickly. He spent hours on end with Jerry Bruno, the advance man for the White House, and cultivated friendships with the Secret Service agents who were assigned to the trip. Beyond Washington figures, he worked with Congressman Jim Wright, state Senator Don Kennard, and other local Democratic Party leaders in Fort Worth and with County Chairman William H. Clark, Connally Campaign Chair Eugene Locke, and other officials in Dallas.

Barnes dedicated many concentrated, intensive weeks of his life to this assignment. In the process, he became a central figure in addressing several issues regarding trip plans, most of which involved planning and politically tweaking events scheduled for Dallas.

First, there had been a loud squabble in Fort Worth when Kennedy loyalists complained that they could not get tickets to the Chamber of Commerce breakfast at the Hotel Texas. That political boilover was resolved by the decision to have President Kennedy address a public rally on a parking lot across the street before the breakfast. However, that quick solution hit a snag: the owner of the parking lot was not a Kennedy fan and was not inclined to make the property available. Only the persuasion of young Fort Worth attorney Dee Kelly, a Connally loyalist and the owner's own lawyer, saved the rally.

In Dallas, community leaders favored the centrally located Dallas Trade Mart as the ideal location for the non-partisan luncheon. But local Democrats lobbied for the Women's Building at Fair Park, which would have accommodated a larger crowd of supporters. With building owner John Stemmons, a cochairman of the luncheon, donating use of the hall, the community leaders prevailed.

And then there were differences surrounding the motorcade. The White House favored it because it provided the best opportunity for the public to physically experience the president and first lady in person. Other voices opposed any sort of motorcade for the obvious security reasons that arose from that sort of exposure. Governor and Mrs. Connally also were opposed, but not for security reasons. Their concern was for preserving the energy of the first couple, knowing from experience that responding to crowds in a motorcade is a taxing exercise, both physically and emotionally.

There also was the related question of whether to publish the motorcade route. Senator Yarborough and the White

House favored doing so in order to maximize the crowds, and ultimately they prevailed. Maps of the route appeared in local newspapers several days in advance.

Meanwhile, when he was not representing Connally to referee differences, young Ben Barnes was helping to raise money for the Austin dinner. In their eagerness to recruit Governor Connally to host the Texas trip, White House and party officials had initially offered to take responsibility for ticket sales and fund-raising for the Austin dinner. However, Connally's legislative liaison Larry Temple recalls that it soon became evident that the White House and the National Democratic Party organizations lacked the ability to do so. With the vital fundraising efforts flagging, the governor reluctantly mobilized the Texas Democratic Party and his personal political organization to take over the task.

As noted, while the state was overwhelmingly Democratic in 1963, there was vigorous and sometimes bitter friction between its liberal wing, championed for several years by Senator Yarborough, and the conservative wing, now led by Governor Connally.

Once committed to underwriting the Austin dinner, Connally was not hesitant in using his considerable persuasive powers on moneyed conservative supporters, many of whom were card-carrying Republicans.

"I understand you don't like [the president]," he would say, "and I don't care [using more earthy words] whether you vote for him or not. But we cannot let Texas be embarrassed on this visit." I can personally vouch for the content and tone of those calls as I was sitting next to him when he made them in the Austin office of the State Democratic Executive Committee. I can say without equivocation that John Connally raised the big money for the Kennedy visit with his bare hands, and because of his efforts, the dinner's financial success was ensured.

At the same time, acting as the governor's point person on planning questions and speaking on his behalf to powerful leadership figures across the state did no harm to Barnes's political future.

Barnes would go on to be chosen the youngest Speaker of the Texas House in the history of the state and be elected lieutenant governor four years later with more than 2 million votes, the largest vote total ever recorded for any statewide office. His efforts and successes also came to the attention of Vice President Johnson. His political instincts and boundless energy would later prompt Johnson to predict that Barnes might someday become the president of the United States.

But for now, the young lawmaker would settle just to keep all the wheels in motion on the complex and delicate arrangements that he had helped negotiate for the presidential visit to Texas. In later years, Barnes would be sidelined by a Texas political scandal that denied him the governor's office, even though he was in fact an innocent bystander. He never made it to the presidential arena. Still, half a century later, he remains one of the most influential figures in Washington, D.C.

CHAPTER FOUR

||||||||||||||||||||||||||||||||||||||||||||||||||||||||||||||||||||||||||||||||||||||||||||||||||||||||||||||||||||||||||||||||||

PERHAPS A TRIUMPH IN SIGHT

From the moment Air Force One landed at San Antonio International Airport late in the morning of November 21, 1963, things had clicked off just as planned on the president and first lady's first day in Texas. Governor and Mrs. Connally, Vice President Johnson and Lady Bird, along with a contingent of other dignitaries, had been there to welcome them to the state.

While the vice president and Lady Bird had flown over from their nearby Hill Country ranch, seventeen Texas Democratic members of Congress had come down with the president on Air Force One. More than four dozen members of the Washington Press Corps had followed on the separate Pan American charter flight.

Crowds of citizens—schoolchildren and adults of all ages, ethnicities, and economic levels—lined the San Antonio streets as the president's motorcade made its way to Brooks Air Force Base. There, the president participated in the planned dedication of a new medical research facility before a throng of onlookers.

From that impressively well-attended and warm beginning, the presidential party flew to Houston, where he was the guest of honor that evening for a large and heartfelt tribute to popular Congressman Albert Thomas, a longtime stalwart of the Texas delegation in Washington, who also happened to be chairman of the powerful House Appropriations Committee.

Here too, large and enthusiastic crowds greeted the president and first lady. Before the dinner, Jackie Kennedy delighted a gathering of Mexican Americans by addressing them with remarks in Spanish. It was her only public speaking role on the trip.

Again, it was a good beginning. Now, the president and first lady were on their last lap of a long day, on their way to Fort Worth.

As a well-known Republican, community leader Cornelia (Corky) Friedman never imagined herself meeting a Democratic president late in the evening to welcome him to Fort Worth. But her husband, Bayard Friedman, was mayor of that city, and that was a nonpartisan office.

Accordingly, nearing midnight on the tarmac at Fort Worth's Carswell Air Force Base, Corky found herself doing just that as a dutiful wife.

Still, despite her political predispositions, she clearly remembers the magnetism and charm of the president. "There was a certain air of electricity around him," she recalled.

The Friedmans fulfilled their civic duty as members of the city's hospitality committee, bade their guests good night until the next morning's Chamber of Commerce breakfast, and left for home.

But even as the Friedmans headed for bed, clusters of admirers, despite the late hour, turned out to cheer the presidential caravan all along the roadways into town from the air base. And downtown, a joyful crowd welcomed them as they arrived at the historic Hotel Texas, a favorite local political mecca.

It had been a long and eventful day, but the president and first lady visited with local dignitaries for a while before retiring to Suite 850 upstairs. In fact, the first couple was not supposed to be in those rooms. The hotel management originally had reserved for them the much grander Will Rogers Suite, which Secret Service agents decided to reject for security reasons. That veto resulted in the move to Suite 850, which was far from sumptuous. Vice President and Lady Bird Johnson were reassigned to the Will Rogers Suite.

Upon hearing about the impending switch, host committee members, appalled at the prospect of accommodations not befitting their distinguished guests, went to work. A group of local arts patrons, led by Ruth Carter Johnson, daughter of *Fort Worth Star-Telegram* publisher Amon G. Carter, quickly redecorated the modestly furnished rooms. They assembled sixteen pieces of world-class art and sculpture and arranged them artistically in the nondescript suite, transforming it into a special cultural experience. Their guests were so touched by the gesture that the president telephoned to thank Ruth Carter Johnson personally the next morning while she was at home with a sick child. It was thought to be one of the last phone calls Kennedy ever made.

With the first couple safe within their suite, Secret Service agents themselves retired for relaxation nearby at The Cellar, a celebrated club frequented by local politicians.

As the Kennedys prepared for bed, Governor Connally was still at work, holding court with old friends in the coffee shop downstairs, as he often did when in his home city. In fact, this was the very same coffee shop where he had invited me to join his initial campaign for governor almost two years earlier.

That night I sat with Connally as he bantered with *Houston Chronicle* political writer Bo Byers about a poll to be published in the newspaper on the following Sunday. Byers was coy about its findings but finally teased that it would show the governor only "slightly ahead of the president" in popularity in Texas.

Spirits were high that night after a successfully executed and gratifying first day of the tour. Tomorrow morning the hotel ballroom would be jammed for the Fort Worth Chamber of Commerce breakfast that Chamber President Raymond Buck had begged both the president and the vice president to have included on the schedule. In advance of that, many more who could not get tickets to the breakfast would hear and see the president at a brief rally across the street in the "Republican" parking lot.

Only a few miles east, preparations were in place for 2,400 luncheon guests to see and hear President Kennedy and First Lady Jacqueline Kennedy at the Dallas Trade Mart.

Connally initially had not wanted to bring the president to Dallas, according to former Dallas mayor Erik Jonsson, feeling that it was not a good political fit. However, when the White House persisted, Connally relented, using his considerable influence with the city's power structure to shape the nonpartisan luncheon sponsored by the three preeminent community organizations.

Jonsson was mindful of past embarrassing episodes

surrounding visits to Dallas by prominent Democratic political figures. On one occasion Lyndon Johnson, then majority leader, and Lady Bird had been heckled and spat at there during the 1960 presidential campaign. And United Nations Ambassador Adlai Stevenson was harassed, physically accosted, and struck during an appearance in the city only weeks before the president's visit. In view of those incidents, legendary merchant Stanley Marcus of the Neiman Marcus stores personally had advised President Kennedy not to come to Dallas.

In response to those concerns, luncheon chairman Jonsson had convened several meetings of Dallas security authorities to be certain of adequate security measures. He was not pleased with the luncheon site itself because of its numerous entrances. But after extended discussions with law enforcement officials, Jonsson was reassured and even optimistic that the day would go well in Dallas.

Two hundred miles to the south, Connally forces in Austin had completed a busy day planning for their events in the capital city slated for Friday. The governor had turned to trusted aide Larry Temple to make arrangements for the important reception at the Governor's Mansion, where the Kennedys would meet members of the Texas Legislature and other state officials.

But Temple had a small problem.

The elegant Governor's Mansion had been cloaked in a misty rain all afternoon, and it was not roomy enough to accommodate the entire anticipated crowd inside. To make matters worse, there was no other adjacent covered space.

The obvious answer, Temple decided, was to rent a tent. Unfortunately, there was no suitable tent available in Austin, and it was too late to obtain one from Houston or Dallas.

Not to be stymied by logistics, the innovative Temple called on a friendly funeral director to loan a large tent. He remembers thinking to have the flaps of the tent folded under to obscure the name of the mortuary. Nevertheless, "It was still a green funeral tent," he lamented.

A few blocks away, Will D. Davis, a rising young attorney and member of the State Democratic Executive Committee, had spent the day reviewing arrangements for the epic gala and fund-raising dinner that was to culminate the president's visit to Texas. It was a task that he had been personally assigned by Governor Connally. The extensive decorations were all in place at Austin's Municipal Auditorium, the largest venue in town. Famed Texas caterer Walter Jetton of Fort Worth would start cooking the steaks that guests would consume at the $100-a-plate dinner. Some guests were already making their way to Austin from towns all across the state.

At the State Capitol, Barnes was fielding questions from legislators about the upcoming reception at the Governor's Mansion and the dinner that night. At the same time, he juggled a constant barrage of calls from the White House advance team members.

Downtown, Neal Spelce, the well-known news director for KTBC television and radio, had been meeting with Austin Police Chief R. E. Miles to coordinate his broadcast coverage plans for the day's big events. He was especially concerned about all arrangements since Vice President Johnson and Lady Bird were the owners of KTBC, then the only television station in Austin.

The Johnsons had plans of their own to complete, since the Kennedys' grand tour of Texas was to conclude with an overnight stay at the LBJ Ranch, with a big barbecue to be held on the banks of the Pedernales River the next day. President Kennedy had been to the ranch only once before, during the 1960 presidential campaign. His brother Robert Kennedy, the attorney general-to-be, came with him on that occasion, and both got the classic Johnson treatment, riding around the ranch in his yellow Lincoln convertible. James Davis, the former butler and ranch house generalissimo, also remembers with a chuckle that the future attorney general got a rude introduction to the hunting culture of Texas. A novice at the sport, he failed to hold his gun properly and sustained a mean jolt to his face from the recoil. Davis recalls that beyond a few snickers there wasn't much said about it at the time.

But this visit was of a different sort. Kennedy was now president and thus was Johnson's superior. Therefore, it was no surprise that all ranch hands were on deck checking out preparations to ensure that the president and first lady experienced all of the charm of the Texas Hill Country.

Lady Bird Johnson herself was so determined that the visit would be perfect that she dispatched her personal secretary, Bess Abell, and her Washington household staff couple, Helen and Gene Williams, to Texas to oversee arrangements. The ranch was abuzz with preparations, Abell remembers.

The White House Communications Signal Corps sent a detachment to route telephone lines through the trees so that the president could have instant communications with the White House and world leaders.

Secret Service agents ran here and there setting up multiple checkpoints.

Ranch cook Mary Davis had been experimenting with different recipes for cream of corn soup, reported to be a favorite of the president. Meanwhile, butler James Davis puzzled over the appropriate glass in which to serve champagne on the rocks, rumored to be the first lady's favored drink. A spread of Hill Country pies and loaves of homemade bread crowded kitchen countertops, all ready to go into the oven at the appointed time. And to cater to another interest of the first lady, quality horses had been brought in to provide her the option of a morning ride.

To help complete sleeping arrangements, James Davis was awaiting the arrival of a special mattress and backboard that always accompanied President Kennedy to accommodate his chronic back problems.

Barbecue king Jetton and his crew had already arrived and fired up the coals for Saturday's luncheon feast. Popular humorist Cactus Pryor, a star personality on the Johnsons' broadcast stations, was finishing the script for a folksy entertainment program segment to highlight the afternoon festivities.

Abell clearly remembers that the most adamant instruction that she had been given by Vice President Johnson when he left for San Antonio was, "Do not let me bring the president in through the kitchen." She explained that people usually entered that way, because it was the most convenient entrance from the airstrip and parking area at the rear of the house.

"You'd go in past the laundry and the ironing boards and the ice machine and the beer keg and then go through the kitchen and into the more gracious and welcoming part of the house," said Abell.

"Don't let me do that," Johnson underscored. "I want to be able to bring them in through the den or the living room."

A relaxing night in the informal atmosphere of the Hill Country was planned as a counterpoint to the exciting but grueling two days. Perhaps, it was hoped, the two men might forge a closer relationship while together, off the public stage.

The following day, after a leisurely morning, the first couple would enjoy the disarming charm of a traditional Texas barbecue under a canopy of live oaks on the banks of the peaceful Pedernales River. Everything was arranged to produce an experience they never would forget.

||||||||||||||||||||||||||||||||||||||||||||||||||||||||||||||||||||||||||||||||||||||||||||||||||||||||||||||

CHAPTER FIVE

THE LAST BREAKFAST IN FORT WORTH

As I awaited arrival of the presidential party amid the expectant chatter of hundreds of guests inside the Hotel Texas ballroom, I realized that I was standing near where I had begun my journey with Governor Connally almost two years earlier.

Only a few hundred feet away in an office building across the street, I worked with him on his Democratic primary campaign throughout the spring and summer of 1962 as he led the popular vote over five opponents. After that primary victory, we moved the campaign headquarters to Austin for the general election in which he won the governorship. We had tasted the sweetness of victory then, and the large crowd assembled here in this ballroom today seemed a harbinger of another Connally triumph.

Earlier that morning, I had already heard President Kennedy give one rousing speech.

Local Democrats, with the help of Connally troubleshooter Barnes, had persuaded the White House to schedule Kennedy to address a large crowd of cheering supporters, which he did under a drizzling sky on a parking lot across the street from the hotel. As I watched the president standing in front of Governor Connally, Vice President Johnson, House Speaker Jim Wright, and local state Senator Don Kennard, I allowed myself a brief flush of pride at the realization that I had handled political campaigns for three of those five elected leaders.

Back inside the hotel, members of the Fort Worth business community, led by Chamber president and power broker Buck, packed the room. The official party was about to enter and the air of expectation grew stronger, as did the crowd's murmurs. Men in the audience were curious to see and hear the handsome young Democratic president, no matter their personal politics, or his.

But just as many of Fort Worth's best-dressed ladies were also there, eager to catch a glimpse of the glamorous first lady. What would she choose to wear for this important day?

In the kitchen adjacent to the ballroom, Mayor Friedman and his wife, Corky, waited with the other hosts and head table guests for their time to enter and be seated. Corky remembers that Vice President Johnson seemed morose and silent, pacing impatiently back and forth. In sharp contrast, she observed, Lady Bird Johnson talked almost incessantly, perhaps to fill her husband's silence.

It was time to begin, and the dignitaries entered the room to hearty applause. First to enter was President Kennedy, followed by Vice President Johnson and Mrs. Johnson, then Governor Connally and Mrs. Connally, and after them, Senator Ralph Yarborough.

But no Jackie Kennedy.

The president already had joked about her absence at the earlier rally appearance.

"It takes her a bit longer," he had said, "but then she looks a lot better than Lyndon and me."

Mrs. Johnson's assistant, the famed humorist Liz Carpenter, was standing beside me against a wall in the back of the ballroom.

"Do you think she is going to show?" Liz asked.

"Are you kidding?" I replied. "She will make her own grand entrance."

Sure enough, on cue from the event's ringmaster Raymond Buck, Jackie Kennedy entered the room to roaring applause, radiant in her soon-to-be-infamous pink suit and matching pillbox hat. It was a truly triumphant entry, with the predictable effect.

The president's address, laced with prominent mentions of local defense installations dear to Fort Worth, was warmly received. True to Governor Connally's prediction, he was liked by those who saw and heard him.

The breakfast proceeded in good order, and once it was over, I prepared to head for Austin as planned, after telling newsmen that I would see them at the banquet that evening. But once outside, greeted by a clearing blue sky, puffy white clouds, and warming sunshine, my original plan was lost to a sense of euphoria as excitement grew in anticipation for the rest of the day.

I would have plenty of time to finish my work on Governor Connally's introductory remarks for the president before the start of the dinner in Austin tonight, I thought.

So in a fated act, I rejoined the White House Press Corps on the bus, along with a number of local reporters, for the ride back to the chartered press plane and a brief flight to

Dallas to attend the luncheon at the Trade Mart, which was to take place immediately after the motorcade through downtown Dallas.

At the same time following the breakfast, Mayor Friedman and Corky had resumed their host committee roles and returned to Carswell Air Force Base with the Kennedys to see them off on Air Force One for the next short leg of the journey.

As they stood on the tarmac, bidding their famous guests good-bye, Corky heard Jackie's soft voice for the first time as she thanked Chamber President Buck for a gift of Justin cowboy boots. Kennedy himself earlier had twice resisted Buck's urging to don a Stetson cowboy hat gift at the breakfast before finally promising to wear it in Washington.

Jackie was more responsive: "I'll wear them at the [LBJ] ranch tomorrow."

Then, the president complimented Corky Friedman on her earrings.

"I almost fainted," she still gasps.

Well after President Kennedy's death, Bayard Friedman still was touched by Kennedy's magnetism.

"His presence does not leave you for days," Friedman commented.

CHAPTER SIX

||||||||||||||||||||||||||||||||||||||||||||||||||||||||||||||||||||||||||||||||||||||||||||||||||||||||||||||||||||||

THE UNTHINKABLE

As an unofficial host and official representative of Governor Connally, I had taken a seat at the front of the Press Corps bus as we departed Love Field for the motorcade through downtown Dallas. This was the front righthand seat, from which point I happened to have a clear view across the driver onto Dealey Plaza, looking down the incline at the presidential limousine as it rolled past the School Book Depository.

Suddenly, I heard a loud pop. And then two more.

Perhaps a motorcycle backfire, I thought.

But in an instant, I saw a police motorcycle leave the pavement, rapidly mounting the soon-to-be-notorious "grassy knoll" beyond the street. Other police and civilians began to rush around the area in confusion. At the same moment, I saw the limousine carrying the Kennedys and the Connallys bound forward with a lurch and disappear through an underpass.

Clearly something had gone wrong. How desperately wrong, we had no idea.

It must be remembered that on this day—fifty years ago—cell phones were still thirty years in the future. Only a few reporters in a three-person "press pool" ahead of us in the motorcade had radio or radio-telephone contact. Indeed, Merriman Smith of United Press broke the first bulletin that the president and Connally had been shot by commandeering a White House phone from a staff member in the pool car. But his initial report carried no detail of the seriousness of the president's injuries.

Back in the Press Corps bus, with the White House Deputy Press Secretary Kilduff in one of the cars ahead, his assistant, Jiggs Fauver, and I had to decide quickly what to do with the media. While I could not know for sure, the lurching limousine and the panic of the crowd that I saw drove instinct to tell me that there had been an injury and that the limousine probably was headed to a hospital—most likely nearby Parkland Hospital, the primary destination for trauma treatment.

That notwithstanding, without much hesitation, we made the decision to stay within our authority and proceed to our original destination, the Dallas Trade Mart, where the huge luncheon crowd awaited.

If the presidential limo were headed to Parkland, the media would find their way there soon enough, I thought.

During that brief and ominous ride, uncertainty and speculation quickly mounted and grew ever louder aboard the bus. The moment the bus pulled to a halt at the Trade Mart, reporters piled off and raced to the bank of pay telephones, which at that time routinely lined the walls of such public meeting places, to seek any information on what was going on and to report on what they had seen.

I had my own immediate mission. I hurried straight toward the head table to seek out Erik Jonsson, who, as head of the Dallas Citizens Council, was both the lead host and master of ceremonies for the event. I will never forget the eerie feeling of running into that hall and hearing the anticipatory murmur of 2,400 unsuspecting guests awaiting the arrival of President Kennedy.

"Mr. Jonsson," I said to him, as he towered over me from the elevated head table. "We think something terrible has happened to the president and Governor Connally. We don't know for sure, but we think they have been shot."

Jonsson just stared at me for a moment, then said quietly, "I think we will wait for a few minutes."

My message delivered, I raced outside to look for a cab or some other means to get me quickly to Parkland Hospital, where I guessed the limousine had gone. Incredibly, good fortune was with me. I had no more than run out the door of the hall when I encountered the wife of a Fort Worth friend who was arriving in her car for the luncheon. She permitted herself to be commandeered and rushed me to Parkland to look for Nellie and John Connally. I was hoping for anything better than the worst, but the worst was on my mind.

On arriving at Parkland Hospital, I ran toward the nearest entrance. It was an end door, and I remember how surprised I was to find it unlocked and unattended—there actually was no one anywhere in sight. It seemed inconceivable to me that the leader of the free world was inside and there was no evidence of any security whatsoever. I was instantly relieved that we had made the decision to direct the press bus to the Trade Mart. The last thing the hospital needed was a bevy of aggressive reporters to add to the chaos right now, certainly with no security in place.

Unimpeded as I found myself, I rushed inside and began

JFK'S FINAL HOURS IN TEXAS

to search for Nellie Connally. With the help of hospital personnel, I quickly found her on the first floor, seated by herself in a corridor outside of trauma room 2, where her husband of twenty-three years was fighting for his life.

Across the dark hall only a few feet away sat Jackie Kennedy, also unaccompanied, outside of trauma room 1, where her husband was facing even longer odds to survive.

The picture of fashion and elegance in the limousine only half an hour earlier, she still wore the blood-splattered pink suit that only minutes ago brought adoring cheers from throngs of spectators along Dallas sidewalks.

Someone had placed two simple straight chairs in the hallway for the two grieving women. Nellie Connally later said that neither of them spoke, each grappling silently with her own raw emotions.

I never will forget that unreal scene of the two wives, absolutely alone in the dark corridor, silently awaiting the fates of their husbands.

I felt helpless and out of place in their company.

Nellie was remarkably calm under the circumstances, and obviously glad to see a familiar face. She quickly told me that the governor was already undergoing surgery, and that his traveling aide, Bill Stinson, was inside the operating room with him.

However, I needed to learn more—much more—immediately. I was certain that there were only a few minutes before the media would be crawling all over Parkland seeking answers to an international tragedy. I understood that Malcolm Kilduff would soon have to speak regarding the president's condition, the obvious first concern of the White House Press. But I knew that reporters would also want to know the condition of Governor Connally and what had occurred in the motorcade. I was reluctant to question Mrs.

Connally in this hour of crisis, but I urgently felt that I must be able to provide at least some information.

Nellie obviously was deeply fearful about Governor Connally's chances for survival as he lay seriously wounded, surrounded by a team of surgeons just a few feet away beyond the door into trauma room 2. It was too early to have an answer to that question, so I asked her what had happened.

She remained composed as she told me briefly what she had seen, heard, and done as the horror unfolded.

As we stood there in the corridor, Nellie and I constructed a rough sketch of the seating arrangement in the limousine. Governor and Mrs. Connally sat in front, ahead of the president and first lady, respectively. The two in the rear sat in slightly elevated seats to afford better views to the public.

She said that both couples had been genuinely overwhelmed by the warm reception that the president and first lady were receiving from massive crowds lining the streets of downtown Dallas.

"I had just turned to him and said, 'Mr. President, you certainly can't say that Dallas doesn't love you,'" she told me, in a voice still shaking from the experience only minutes before.

Then she described hearing the first shot over their shoulders and, seeing her husband slump, instinctively pulling him down over her lap, an action later credited with saving his life.

"I just didn't want them to hurt him anymore," she said, her eyes moist.

Then she looked away as she described the sickening experience of feeling brain tissue sprinkle the interior of the limousine following the final shot at the president.

Years later, in 1993, she told of her experience in much greater detail in her book, *From Love Field*, written from notes that she scrawled on a legal pad after she and the governor returned home from Parkland Hospital.

As I started to leave, Nellie exclaimed, "Please don't leave me. I am always alone." Torn deeply by her heart-rending vulnerability and grief, I nonetheless explained that I needed to find Malcolm Kilduff to help coordinate handling of the Press Corps that was about to descend on the hospital. With typical grace, she quickly understood the situation and accepted it, then returned to her lonely vigil outside the door.

Shortly afterward I found Kilduff, and we quickly set up a temporary press room in a nurses' training room downstairs from the trauma rooms. We finished none to soon: members of the Press Corps were already arriving.

Rumors were rampant, but hard facts still were scant and elusive. In the midst of this confusion, reporters saw a Catholic priest arrive. Instantly, they inferred that their worst fears about the president were confirmed.

At 1:33 p.m. on November 22, Kilduff stepped before the crowd of reporters in the makeshift press room and announced that the president had died at 1 p.m.

Several minutes later, from his studio in New York City, Walter Cronkite announced the shattering news to the world on the CBS television network, wiping away a speck of a tear as he did so. It was 1:38 p.m. on the wall clock behind his desk.

Moments after Kilduff's announcement, I joined him to speak to reporters. Using a blackboard and chalk, and based on the sketch made in the corridor, I diagrammed the seating arrangement inside the limousine and then relayed Nellie Connally's report regarding what had happened.

It was only the first of numerous briefings and interviews I would conduct in a fog of fatigue and emotion in the course of the following days. It was just the beginning of an ordeal that seemed to have no end in sight.

Only an hour after I stood at the blackboard, Lyndon Baines Johnson was sworn in as the next president of the United States aboard Air Force One at Love Field. His staff and the late president's party, including First Lady Jacqueline Kennedy and the dead president's body, immediately departed for Washington, D.C., leaving Dallas in the distance.

But for those of us who remained on the ground in Dallas, the work was just beginning.

Although Governor Connally's wounds were critical, he was to survive, thanks first to Nellie's instinctive action to pull him down in the car, which served to plug the gaping wound in his lung, and then to the extraordinary work of Dr. Robert Shaw and his Parkland surgical team, who were able to make the lifesaving repairs to the wound. But Connally faced a long recovery and would remain at Parkland for ten days.

I was just beginning to experience full immersion in the ultimate crisis management experience of a lifetime. Even today—fifty years later—it sometimes seems like a bad dream, too incredible to have actually happened.

CHAPTER SEVEN

ENDURING THE PARKLAND MAELSTROM

The completion of my briefing was just the beginning of a long watch that would keep me at Parkland for the next three days. My identification at the briefing podium made me a marked man for questions. No matter whether I had the answers, I was someone visible in a sea of uncertainty.

I continued to field inquiries about Governor Connally's condition all afternoon.

Late in the day, I coordinated a news conference for Dr. Shaw, after he and his team had completed four hours of surgery to save Connally's life. His report that the governor was expected to survive was the best news of the day. (I was astounded to find a YouTube video of that news conference in the fall of 2012.)

In addition to the reporters who were hungry for more information, frantic family members and friends of the Connallys began to surface. Some came in person; many more navigated the hospital switchboard to find me or anyone familiar. Hand-scrawled messages piled up on my make-shift desk. They all wanted to know how "John and Nellie" were doing. What could they do to help? As close friends and supporters, they certainly were entitled to time and attention for their concern, but responding to their sheer numbers filled hours all afternoon. The hospital was awash with distressed people, all needing some attention.

Thankfully, some help simply appeared unsolicited. The nearby Braniff Airways flight kitchen dispatched much-welcomed meals on airliner trays. And a staff member from the downtown Adolphus Hotel walked in and poured out a pile of room keys for Connally family members.

As evening turned into very late night, a new wave of openly distraught journalists appeared on the scene, mostly from Europe, I surmised; they were decidedly non-Texan in their accents.

It was a compelling display of President Kennedy's popularity beyond U.S. shores.

His assassination had brought newspeople from around the globe to Dallas as quickly as they could get there. The city had become an international dateline, but in a manner found to be utterly deplorable.

Throughout the evening, Nellie Connally and the rest of us continued to follow news coverage from Washington on funeral plans for the fallen president. As detailed later in this account, Nellie designated her son John to represent the family for that somber occasion. Others named to represent Texas included Dallasite Eugene Locke, Connally's campaign chairman, and Texas Attorney General Waggoner Carr.

After hours of anguish and uncertainty over her husband's fate, the exhausted Nellie could rest easier now. She could get some fitful sleep in her cubbyhole next to his room with confidence that he should move off the critical list by tomorrow. But she was surprised when a nurse awakened her at 2 a.m. with word that the governor wanted to see her.

It was a sweet reunion, but only momentary, as Connally then asked Nellie to send in an even more surprised Nancy Abington, a close friend who was spending the night with her.

"Please take care of Nellie," the governor told Nancy. "She is always alone."

"It was the sweetest thing I could ever hear," Nellie recalls.

My wife, Anice, and our daughters, Courtney and Ellen, were keeping their own vigil in nearby Fort Worth, knowing that I would not be home for several days. Ellen was so young that she remembers little of those events. But Courtney, who was ill and home from school, saw her dad on television and notified her mother.

It was well after midnight that I finally was able to retire to accommodations provided by the hospital staff in the nurses' quarters in an adjacent building. Though finally alone with my thoughts, I could not grasp all that I had witnessed within the past twelve hours. I wondered what had happened in Austin that night, where hundreds of Texans were to descend on the state capital for the gala fundraising dinner that was to have climaxed the president's trip to Texas. How ironic, I thought, that I never wrote the suggested remarks for Governor Connally's introduction of President Kennedy at that never-to-be gala that was to have taken place a few hours before.

The president, Connally, and Johnson at the White House,
when Connally served Kennedy as Secretary of the Navy.

Kennedy, Jackie, and Nellie Connally leaving the San Antonio airport for Brooks Air Force Base.

First Lady Jackie Kennedy reacts to joyous welcome in San Antonio.

(above) Kennedy speaks to the crowd at Brooks Air Force Base, where he dedicated a new medical facility.

(opposite page) The custom hand-crafted podium the president used in San Antonio is in the collection of the city's Witte Museum.

First Lady Jackie Kennedy speaking in Spanish to Mexican Americans at a League of United Latin American Citizens (LULAC) meeting in Houston.

Fort Worth hosts redecorated the Kennedys' Hotel Texas suite with world-class art. Fifty years later, the art was reassembled by Dallas Museum of Art Associate Director Olivier Meslay and Amon Carter Museum of American Art Director Dr. Andrew Walker for exhibition in their respective museums to honor President Kennedy.

Ben Barnes became speaker of the Texas House of Representatives at age twenty-six.

*Texas barbecue king Walter Jetton had
already fired up the pit at the LBJ Ranch.*

Austin's Municipal Auditorium awaiting people from across Texas to welcome the president at the climactic fund-raising gala.

MUNICIPAL AUDITORIUM & CONVENTION CENTER

WELCOME
PRESIDENT JOHN F KENNEDY

In honor of
President John F. Kennedy
and
Vice President Lyndon B. Johnson

The State Democratic Executive Committee
requests the pleasure of your company
at the
Texas Welcome Dinner
on Friday evening the twenty-second of November
One thousand nine hundred and sixty-three
at half after seven o'clock
at the Municipal Auditorium
in the City of Austin

Contribution card enclosed
Optional dress

Mr. Eugene M. Locke, Chairman
Mrs. Alfred Negley, Vice-Chairman
Mr. Frank C. Erwin, Jr., Secretary

Formal invitation to the $100-a-plate dinner in Austin.

President, United States of America

Vice President, United States of America

Governor, State of Texas

TEXAS WELCOME DINNER

NOVEMBER 22, 1963, MUNICIPAL AUDITORIUM, AUSTIN, TEXAS

 PROGRAM

Eugene M. Locke, Master of Ceremonies, Chairman, State Democratic Executive Committee

Music by Volunteers from The University of Texas Longhorn Band. Vincent R. DiNino, Director.

Entrance of National and State Official Guests at Head Tables

Invocation by Dr. Robert Tate, Minister of the First Methodist Church of Austin

The National Anthem

Introduction of Members of the State Democratic Executive Committee by Eugene M. Locke

Introduction of Members of the Texas House of Representatives by Speaker Byron Tunnell

Introduction of Members of the Texas Senate by Lieutenant Governor Preston Smith

Introduction of Guests at Head Tables by Eugene M. Locke

Entrance of Governor and Mrs. John Connally

Entrance of Vice President and Mrs. Lyndon B. Johnson

Entrance of President and Mrs. John F. Kennedy

Welcome by Governor Connally

Remarks by Vice President Johnson

Address by President Kennedy

Benediction by the Very Reverend Edward C. Matocha, Chancellor of the Diocese of Texas

LYNDON B. JOHNSON

JOHN F. KENNEDY

JOHN CONNALLY

The dinner program for the Austin gala was mailed to ticket holders after Kennedy's death as a memento of the unfulfilled evening.

(above) President Kennedy speaking to a large crowd in a parking lot across from Hotel Texas. Standing behind him (left to right) are state Senator Don Kennard, U.S. Senator Ralph Yarborough, Texas Governor John Connally, and Vice President Lyndon Johnson.

(opposite page) Kennedy reaching out to the Fort Worth crowd following his parking lot address.

View of sold-out audience attending the Fort Worth Chamber of Commerce breakfast on November 22, 1963.

WELCOME MR. KENNEDY
TO DALLAS...

...A CITY so disgraced by a recent Liberal smear attempt that its citizens have just elected two more Conservative Americans to public office.

...A CITY that is an economic "boom town," not because of Federal handouts, but through conservative economic and business practices.

...A CITY that will continue to grow and prosper despite efforts by you and your administration to penalize it for its non-conformity to "New Frontierism."

...A CITY that rejected your philosophy and policies in 1960 and will do so again in 1964 — even more emphatically than before.

MR. KENNEDY, despite contentions on the part of your administration, the State Department, the Mayor of Dallas, the Dallas City Council, and members of your party, we free-thinking and America-thinking citizens of Dallas still have, through a Constitution largely ignored by you, the right to address our grievances, to question you, to disagree with you, and to criticize you.

In asserting this constitutional right, we wish to ask you publicly the following questions—indeed, questions of paramount importance and interest to all free peoples everywhere—which we trust you will answer . . . in public, without sophistry. These questions are:

WHY is Latin America turning either anti-American or Communistic, or both, despite increased U. S. foreign aid, State Department policy, and your own Ivy-Tower pronouncements?

WHY do you say we have built a "wall of freedom" around Cuba when there is no freedom in Cuba today? Because of your policy, thousands of Cubans have been imprisoned, are starving and being persecuted—with thousands already murdered and thousands more awaiting execution and, in addition, the entire population of almost 7,000,000 Cubans are living in slavery.

WHY have you approved the sale of wheat and corn to our enemies when you know the Communist soldiers "travel on their stomachs" just as ours do? Communist soldiers are daily wounding and or killing American soldiers in South Viet Nam.

WHY did you host, salute and entertain Tito — Moscow's Trojan Horse — just a short time after our sworn enemy, Khrushchev, embraced the Yugoslav dictator as a great hero and leader of Communism?

WHY have you urged greater aid, comfort, recognition, and understanding for Yugoslavia, Poland, Hungary, and other Communist countries, while turning your back on the pleas of Hungarian, East German, Cuban and other anti-Communist freedom fighters?

WHY did Cambodia kick the U.S. out of its country after we poured nearly 400 Million Dollars of aid into its ultra-leftist government?

WHY has Gus Hall, head of the U.S. Communist Party praised almost every one of your policies and announced that the party will endorse and support your re-election in 1964?

WHY have you banned the showing at U.S. military bases of the film "Operation Abolition"—the movie by the House Committee on Un-American Activities exposing Communism in America?

WHY have you ordered or permitted your brother Bobby, the Attorney General, to go soft on Communists, fellow-travelers, and ultra-leftists in America, while permitting him to persecute loyal Americans who criticize you, your administration, and your leadership?

WHY are you continuing the U.S. continuing to give economic aid to Argentina, in spite of that fact that Argentina has just seized almost 400 Million Dollars of American private property?

WHY has the Foreign Policy of the United States degenerated to the point that the C.I.A. is arranging coups and having staunch Anti-Communist Allies of the U.S. bloodily exterminated.

WHY have you scrapped the Monroe Doctrine in favor of the "Spirit of Moscow"?

MR. KENNEDY, as citizens of these United States of America, we DEMAND answers to these questions, and we want them NOW.

THE AMERICAN FACT-FINDING COMMITTEE
"An unaffiliated and non-partisan group of citizens who wish truth"

BERNARD WEISSMAN,
Chairman

P.O. Box 1792 — Dallas 21, Texas

(opposite page) The president and first lady with Texas Governor John Connally and Nellie Connally deplaning Air Force One at Love Field.

(above) President Kennedy had been greeted in Dallas by a full-page advertisement that viciously attacked him.

Kennedy leaves his security force to greet the crowd at Love Field.

The presidential limousine leaving Love Field.

As the Kennedys and Connallys roll down Main Street in downtown Dallas, cheering crowds shower them with confetti, prompting Nellie Connally to exclaim, "Mr. President, you certainly can't say that Dallas doesn't love you."

The White House Press Corps bus rolls past the School Book Depository seconds after the president is shot, as terrified Dealey Plaza spectators scatter.

White House Deputy Press Secretary Malcolm Kilduff announces the president's death to newsmen in a makeshift press room at 1:33 p.m.

Governor Connally's press aide Julian Read briefs reporters on Nellie Connally's account of what occurred in the presidential limousine.

The notorious Texas School Book Depository, hiding place for Kennedy's assassin, with the sixth floor open window from which the shots were fired.

Texas School Book Depository, November 22, 1963. View of Dealey Plaza from the sixth floor window. Photographer Flip Schulke photographed Lee Harvey Oswald's perch for Life *magazine within hours of the assassination, arriving in the room only fifteen minutes after authorities removed Oswald's rifle.*

CHAPTER EIGHT

THE UNFINISHED ITINERARY

Volumes have been written about all that happened following the assassination in Dallas shortly after noon on Friday, November 22, 1963.

But little has been recorded about the realities that developed in the wake of the event that changed everything. The things that did *not* happen over the remaining hours of the unfinished itinerary and the heartbreak that followed make their own stories.

The most immediate and severe hammer blow fell on the more than 2,400 unsuspecting guests at the nonpartisan luncheon who were awaiting the president at the Dallas Trade Mart, barely a mile away from where his lifeless body lay at Parkland Hospital.

Moments after I expressed to master of ceremonies Erik Jonsson our fears of what had happened to the president and Governor Connally, word began to seep throughout the room. But unsure of the facts, Jonsson waited to verify what had actually happened before he announced to the crowded room that the two leaders had been hit. After making that announcement, he then asked minister Luther Holcomb, who had been scheduled to deliver the invocation, to lead the assemblage in prayer, after which Jonsson called on guests to await further information.

The happy murmur of anticipation in the hall turned to an undertone of anxiety amid whispers and increasing sounds of weeping. Community leaders huddled nervously around the head table, uncertain of what to do next. Eerily, in the background, the entire scene was playing out on live television over KRLD-TV and CBS, with the voice of newsman Eddie Barker offering sporadic and cautious commentary.

It was a score of minutes later before Jonsson drew himself back up to the microphone to confirm the reports, and asked for a concluding prayer. With that, the crowd of Dallas's most powerful citizens began silently to melt away, helpless in spite of their depth of experience against the gut-wrenching tragedy that had enveloped them.

Television viewers watched as a White House aide silently walked to the head table and removed the presidential seal that hung from the podium. A waiter for the event wiped away tears with a napkin as he collected flowers and untouched dishes from the luncheon tables.

As the hall began to empty, Jonsson and a handful of the Citizens Council members adjourned to a nearby office of John Stemmons, who had made his Trade Mart available for the event. There, they urgently began to attempt to get a handle on the madness that had descended upon them. Phone lines were jammed. Solid information was hard to come by. One report pronounced that Governor Connally had also been killed.

It was shortly after the noon hour, and Jonsson would not get home until eight that night. The next day, at his home, he organized an emergency committee to chart a course of action in response to the tragedy. He remembers that he got plenty of advice. His phone never stopped ringing. Stanley Marcus called from New York and suggested, "You ought to have a sunrise service for the president out at the Cotton Bowl."

"Try again, Stanley," Jonsson responded. "We'll not have any meetings of any size anywhere if we can help it."

Of more immediate concern was to respond rapidly to some reliable information that Catholic church congregations were planning to parade from City Hall to the county courthouse. Concerned that such a gathering could foment even more unrest in what was a potentially explosive situation, Jonsson managed to get the required parade permit withdrawn. Fearful for the security of suspected killer Lee Harvey Oswald, Jonsson and his associates made arrangements for him to be transferred from the city jail to the more secure county jail. Two days later, while that transfer was being made, Oswald would be murdered by Jack Ruby before the horrified eyes of the nation on live television, adding another level of depth to the chaos that enveloped Dallas's leadership.

Jonsson could not believe the collapse he was witnessing. What else could possibly happen?

On Sunday, November, 24, Marcus called again from New York, where the Dallas Cowboys were playing the New York Giants, a game that went on in spite of the tragedy. He reported that fans were calling the score: Giants 14, Assassins 0.

Obviously, strong and visible steps had to be taken toward recovery, and as a first gesture to the fallen president and his family, Jonsson and three other leaders courageously traveled to Washington to attend the memorial parade. Jonsson was a giant of the Dallas community, willing to do anything to redeem his beloved city, but in these early days, he had no idea of the depth and extent of the role that awaited him in the long journey back for Dallas specifically and Texas in general.

Thirty-two miles to the west of Dallas, Fort Worth Chamber of Commerce President Raymond Buck, a prominent insurance executive, was plunged into deep depression at the shocking news. Only hours earlier, after all, he had presided over a triumphant high point of the Texas tour. Now, having been one of the civic leaders who had pleaded with the president to come to Fort Worth and other Texas cities, he felt a personal responsibility for his death. His despondency was so deep that he refused to go in to his office for three months, according to his daughter, Kay Buck McDermott.

Texans from all over the state already were in their Austin hotels or on their way by midday on Friday, November 22. State officials and especially their wives had been planning for weeks what they would wear to the reception for President Kennedy and First Lady Jacqueline Kennedy at the Governor's Mansion that afternoon and the fund-raising gala at Municipal Auditorium that evening.

State Democratic Executive Committee member Will Davis was finally satisfied with all the arrangements. He was especially pleased that the fund-raising goal had been reached, thanks to heavy lifting by Governor Connally and Representative Barnes.

Davis now could contemplate the exciting evening ahead that would make it all worth the effort.

And then, in an instant, it was all for naught.

"I was sitting in a barber's chair at the Commodore Perry

Hotel," Davis remembers, "when one of the Secret Service agents I had been working with rushed in out of breath and said he had to report to Dallas at once; 'the president has been shot.'"

Across Austin, radios and television sets crackled with the unbelievable news, along with word that Governor Connally also had been hit and was in critical condition.

Shock turned to disbelief and then to grief. Total strangers exchanged hugs amid tears.

Stunned as he was, Davis and his staff quickly had to go through the sorrowful job of undoing all of their plans for the dinner. The caterer's cooks had been at work for hours. The mountain of food went to charity.

Ben Barnes will never forget the moment he heard the news. He was having lunch with Vice President Johnson's aide Bill Moyers and State Democratic Executive Committee Secretary Frank Erwin at the Forty Acres Club, just off the University of Texas campus. They were reviewing the program for the gala that evening when Moyers received a call.

"Bill had been taking calls all day," Barnes said. "But this one was different. I never had seen such a look of shock and horror on anyone's face."

The president was in critical condition, the caller said, and Johnson wanted Moyers to be at Love Field in Dallas as quickly as he could get there.

Barnes grabbed another phone, called Colonel Homer Garrison, head of the Texas Department of Public Safety, explained the crisis, and asked for a DPS aircraft. Only minutes later, Moyers was on his way to Dallas to take his place in the drama that was soon to follow, as President Kennedy was pronounced dead and Lyndon Johnson was sworn in on Air Force One as his successor.

Not far across town, KTBC television news director Neal Spelce was having lunch with Austin Police Chief Miles again for one last review of coverage plans for the afternoon, when his own staff member interrupted with the news. Spelce had just been fretting that he did not have enough cameras to cover the presidential motorcade in from the airport. It did not matter now.

While the rest of the world understandably was focused on the president's death, millions of Texans, most especially those who had plans to attend the Austin festivities, were deeply concerned about the condition of popular Governor Connally, who lay critically wounded at Parkland Hospital.

One Texan who had particular concern for Connally's condition was Lieutenant Governor Preston Smith, who would take over the chief executive's position if Connally became incapacitated.

Connally family friend Nancy Abington remembers that she was tasked with picking up the staunchly conservative Smith and his wife at the airport earlier in the day and making sure they would attend the activities. (Smith had shown signs of wavering.) But now, he was very evident on the scene.

Connally Executive Assistant Howard Rose still chuckles when he recalls Smith's heightened interest.

"If Lieutenant Governor Smith came to my office once that afternoon to inquire about Connally's condition, he must have come half a dozen times," he said.

By late afternoon, reports following hours of surgery indicated that Connally would survive.

Larry Temple no longer had to worry about a presidential reception at the Governor's Mansion, and Will Davis had no gala dinner to manage. But there still was a very large number of grieving Texans in town with no outlet for raw emotions.

Ben Barnes, as an officer of the House of Representatives, went to Speaker Byron Tunnell and proposed that a prayer service be scheduled in the House chamber that evening. Tunnell, though a strong conservative, already had been smitten by Kennedy's charm when the two had met the day before. He told Barnes, "Just go do it."

So Barnes planned and carried out a prayer service in the House chamber that evening, mourning the sadness of the day, and hundreds of Texans gathered there in a somber vigil instead of a gala celebration. The grieving crowd had to settle for crude programs hastily run off on an office mimeograph machine.

At the LBJ Ranch, Bess Abell was down at the barbecue grounds with catering king Walter Jetton and humorist Cactus Pryor, checking on preparations for the next day's big event that would conclude the presidential trip to Texas.

She looked up to see Helen Williams running from the back door of the house down the hill toward them.

"The president has been shot!" she shouted.

The telephones in the house were temporarily down, and the Signal Corps lines to the outside world were not yet operational, so everyone crowded into the kitchen and watched Walter Cronkite announce the president's death on a small black-and-white TV, amid stacks of pecan pies and freshly baked bread.

Abell saw on the television report that the Johnsons were heading back to Washington, D.C., with Mrs. Kennedy and the president's body. She knew that she would be needed immediately. She commandeered the LBJ broadcasting company plane to reach a connecting flight in Dallas and she, accompanied by the Williams couple, rushed back to Washington with the Johnsons' wardrobe on board with them. She found herself surprised to be met at Dulles airport in the middle of the night by a car from the White House, an instant reminder of who her new employer was.

Back at the LBJ Ranch, the Signal Corps crew began to pull down their wires and to pack for departure. Walter Jetton's barbecue crew silently banked the already glowing coals.

There would be no cream of corn soup or champagne served, and there would be no need for the special mattress and backboard in the bedroom. The president was not coming.

||||||||||||||||||||||||||||||||||||||||||||||||||||||||||||||||||||||||||||||||||||||||||||||||||||||||||||||

CHAPTER NINE

LADY BIRD JOHNSON REMEMBERS

M rs. Lyndon B. Johnson, wife of the then vice president, and most often known as Lady Bird, was noted for her practice of maintaining a diary of daily experiences. It was a consistent routine that she had maintained since Lyndon Johnson's early days as a young congressman.

That she took time from the chaos and anguish of November 22 to preserve her thoughts was therefore no surprise. The soft and kind words of her tape-recorded entries now are available to the public at the LBJ Presidential Library and Museum in Austin, Texas.

Her witness of that day starts with the innocent words, "It all began so beautifully. The streets were lined with people—lots of people—the children were smiling, placards, confetti, people waving from windows."

She then relates a riveting account: first, of hearing shots overhead, followed by a stark radio command saying, "Let's get out of here," and seeing Secret Service agent Rufus

Youngblood leap over the limousine's front seat to pin the vice president to the floor, shielding him with his body.

She describes a wild ride to Parkland Hospital.

"As we ground to a halt, Secret Service men began to pull, lead, guide, and hustle us out. I cast one last look over my shoulder and saw in the president's car a bundle of pink, just like a drift of blossoms, lying on the back seat. I think it was Mrs. Kennedy, lying over the president's body."

She describes Lyndon Johnson as being remarkably calm and quiet. Although the fate of President Kennedy was not yet known, Lady Bird Johnson feared the worst, from seeing the face of Kenny O'Donnell, one of his closest aides.

"You better go see if you can see Jackie and Nellie," Lyndon Johnson said.

A Secret Service agent led her up one corridor's back stairs and down another.

"Suddenly, I found myself face to face with Jackie in a small hall," relates Mrs. Johnson. "I think it was just outside the operating room. You always think of her—or someone like her—being insulated, protected; she was quite alone. I don't think I ever saw someone so much alone in my life. I went up to her, put my arms around her and said something to her. I am sure it was something like, 'God, help us all,' because my feelings for her were too tumultuous to put into words.

"And then, I went to see Nellie. There it was different because Nellie and I have gone through many things together since 1938. I hugged her tight, and we both cried and I said, 'Nellie, it's going to be all right.' And Nellie said, 'Yes, John is going to be all right.'

"Then I turned and went back to the small white room where Lyndon was. Mr. [Malcolm] Kilduff and Kenny O'Donnell were coming and going. I think it was Kenny's face and Kenny's voice that I first heard the words, 'The president is dead.'

"Mr. Kilduff entered the room and said to Lyndon, 'Mr. President.'"

Lady Bird Johnson was deeply touched by Jackie Kennedy's kindness over the next few days in spite of the awful burden she carried.

As they shared the cabin of Air Force One returning to Washington with the president's body, "she made it as easy as possible. She would says things like, 'Oh, Lady Bird, it's so good that we've always liked you two so much.' She said, 'Oh, what if I had not been there. I'm so glad I was there.'"

The new first lady again expressed admiration for Mrs. Kennedy on Sunday after she and now-President Johnson accompanied her and Robert Kennedy to the Capitol in Washington where President Kennedy's body lay in state. Lady Bird described it as a day she never would forget.

She remembered how carefully Jackie knelt and kissed her husband's casket with young daughter Caroline by her side.

"To me, one of the saddest things in the whole tragedy was that Mrs. Kennedy achieved, on this desperate day, a state of love, a state of rapport between her and the people of this country.

"Her behavior from the moment of the shot until I said good-bye to her the other day is, to me, one of the most memorable things of all. Maybe it's a combination of great breeding, great discipline, great character. I only know it's great."

CHAPTER TEN

||||||||||||||||||||||||||||||||||||||||||||||||||||||||||||||||||||||||||||||||||||||||||||||||||||||||||||||||||||||

THE CONNALLY
CHILDREN RECALL

John B. Connally III, eldest son of Governor John Connally, was sitting in his bookkeeping class at Austin High School when a school assistant came into the room and asked him to come to the principal's office.

When he was asked to sit down across from the principal, he noticed him dialing up and down the stations on a portable radio.

"And then he said, 'John, I have some bad news,'" Connally remembers. Minutes later, a guard from the Governor's Mansion picked up John, and they raced to Casis Elementary School to pick up his younger brother, Mark.

Only eleven years old at the time, Mark at first wasn't sure why a trooper and his brother would come to get him. The mood inside the car was quiet until they reached nearby O. Henry Junior High.

There they found their weeping and near-hysterical sister, Sharon, hurrying out of the building. Only minutes before, she and friends had been entering the cafeteria for lunch. She noticed that fellow students were staring at her. At that moment, the principal and a counselor approached and asked her to accompany them to the office. As they closed the door to the office, she wondered what she had done wrong.

"Sharon, President Kennedy and your father have been shot."

"To me, 'shot' meant 'dead,'" she said. And then the principal told her that her brothers and a trooper were on their way to get her.

School chum Libby Drake walked with her to retrieve a coat in her locker. A passing boy, unable to see Sharon's face, yelled to Libby, "The president and Governor Connally both are dead." Sharon just sat down and started sobbing.

Once the children were reunited in the car, John assured them that the boy was wrong, and that their dad probably was going to be all right, although he still was undergoing critical surgery at Parkland.

As the children arrived from school, family members including their grandmother, Katie Brill, and friends including Lynda Bird Johnson were already gathering at the Governor's Mansion, many of them having just arrived in Austin to prepare for the festivities planned for that night.

But now, mourning had already begun in the wake of the tragic news from Dallas.

"I remember that when we got to the Mansion, there was a crowd of people milling around inside, and they were all crying," said Mark. "At my age, I was not used to seeing grown people cry, and it bothered me a lot."

They prayed for the governor and the president.

Older brother John headed straight for the downstairs phone and tried to call his mother at Parkland Hospital. He remembers that a young operator trying to assist him was crying. Without knowing to whom she was talking, she said, "I heard that one of them died."

"I was afraid to ask which one," John said. In a moment, she eased the concern for his father, but John still was traumatized by learning the fate of the president.

A short time later, Nellie Connally called the Mansion and talked to young John. She confirmed that his father was still alive, although in critical condition, and at that moment was undergoing what was to become four hours of surgery.

John told his mother that he was going to join her in Dallas. "No," she said, "you need to stay there with your sister and brother." But he insisted on being by her side, and she acquiesced. Sharon and Mark wanted to go, too. But their mother stood firm in saying that they would have to wait for another day.

Howard Rose arranged for a state plane to be available, and John dashed off to Dallas along with Nancy Abington and Nancy Negley, two close friends whom Nellie had requested come to Dallas to be with her.

The quick trip to see his mother was just the start of a progression of surreal experiences awaiting elder son John. After the announcement of the president's death, the White House had asked Nellie Connally whether she would be attending funeral services on Monday. She declined, explaining that the governor's condition was still too serious for her to leave him.

Instead, she suggested that John III attend to represent the family. The Johnsons quickly embraced that idea and made him part of their official party for the Washington, D.C., arrangements. He recalls that at that time, he did not even own a topcoat; Austin clothier Dick Reynolds was kind enough to open up his Congress Avenue store on Sunday for John to select one.

Though only seventeen years old and still shaken by the events, John nevertheless had the presence of mind to urge his mother to write a note of condolence to Mrs. Kennedy. After hesitating about what to say, she did so:

Dear Jackie,

With all my heart, I long to be with you today. John's condition is still too serious for me to leave.

We just want you to know how much we care as we share your grief and join you in prayer.

John and I send you our love.

Nellie Connally
Saturday, November 23, 1963

CHAPTER ELEVEN

||||||||||||||||||||||||||||||||||||||||||||||||||||||||||||||||||||||||||||||||||||||||||||||||||||||||||||||||||||||||||||

THE TRAGEDY LIVED ON

Saturday morning at Parkland confirmed that all that had happened was not just a bad dream.

Newspaper headlines, radios, and television screens still screamed the shock that we had just lived through and continued to face.

Evidence of the nightmare continued to abound. Armed state troopers seemed to be everywhere.

Still uncertain about a possible larger security threat, they had painted the hospital windows black in Governor Connally's area and had installed thick steel plates to deflect any incoming gunfire. News coverage was replete with eyewitness accounts from Dealey Plaza the day before, reports of plans for memorial services for the fallen president, and reactions from around the globe.

We dealt with an increasing number of reporters. Even though I had provided an account of Nellie Connally's experience just after the announcement of President Kennedy's death, there were now mounting calls for a personal statement from her.

George Christian, a respected former Capitol newsman who recently had joined Governor Connally's office as press secretary, had come up from Austin as my reinforcement, and we were working on a statement for Mrs. Connally to make to reporters.

Upon arrival, George was shocked to hear the ever-gracious Governor Connally, his arm high in a sling and tubes protruding, courteously introduce the two of us to his nurse. Reluctant and nervous as she was to speak to the press, Nellie stood tall and faced them on Sunday morning, trembling at a podium as she described the horrible scene in the limousine. She took special pains to express concern for the widow of a Dallas police officer who had been killed by Lee Harvey Oswald, the suspected assassin of the president. As a mountain of floral arrangements already overflowed their rooms, she suggested that sympathizers direct memorial contributions to the officer's family rather than sending more flowers to her and the governor.

(Howard Rose, Connally's executive assistant who came to Dallas to set up a temporary governor's office, recalls that he actually received a letter from a florists' association protesting Mrs. Connally's advice.)

Nellie Connally had just finished her statement and we were watching coverage of the Kennedy memorial activities in Washington on a tiny black-and-white television set in Governor Connally's room when the coverage switched to the scene in the basement of the Dallas city jail, where suspected assassin Lee Harvey Oswald was being transferred from the city jail to the county jail.

Then, to our astonishment, we, along with the rest of the world, watched an obscure nightclub owner named Jack

Ruby step out of the crowd with a pistol and, on live television, fatally shoot Oswald before our eyes.

Minutes later, we heard a commotion in the hallway at Parkland and looked out to watch with disbelief as Oswald was wheeled past us on his way to the emergency room. It was the same room in which President Kennedy had died a scant two days earlier.

I will never forget that Oswald was as green as a gourd. We all could not believe what we were seeing and hearing. Was it never to end?

On Monday, November 25, the Connallys watched President Kennedy's televised funeral services, straining to get a glimpse of their son John, who was there to represent them.

John had been invited to stay with the Johnsons at The Elms, the vice president's residence in Washington, D.C. On Sunday evening he accompanied President Johnson's daughter Luci and her Secret Service agents to view the slain president's casket in the rotunda of the Capitol. He remembers the long lines of mourners circling the block.

The next morning John rode with the Johnsons in their limousine to the White House, which was still occupied by Jackie Kennedy. There, he experienced the first of two sensations that remain indelible after half a century. He recalls both in a chapter of his mother's book, *From Love Field*, published in 2003.

Like most people, John was accustomed to deferring to the family of the deceased at a funeral. So, as he joined the Johnsons in walking out the front of the White House facing Pennsylvania Avenue, he was shocked to see the Kennedy family standing in the driveway waiting for them. Even in their dark hour of anguish, it was they who were showing the traditional deference due the president of the United States.

In like manner, on the other side of the driveway stood 150 heads of state and diplomats from around the world, paying respects with their presence.

John joined the others and they all walked in procession from the White House to St. Matthew's Cathedral for the Funeral Mass.

From there, the procession rode in cars to Arlington National Cemetery for the graveside service. John experienced a second memorable shock when the Johnsons took him with them toward the Kennedys' limousine.

Mrs. Kennedy was inside the car. As they approached, John assumed that the window would roll down, and they would lean over and pay their respects. Instead, he was startled to see her and Attorney General Robert Kennedy open the door and get out of the car to greet them.

"President and Mrs. Johnson shook hands with Attorney General Kennedy and Mrs. Kennedy and expressed their condolences," John writes. "They introduced me to the attorney general, who shook my hand and nodded. His face was ashen and tear-streaked and virtually without expression.

"They then introduced me to Mrs. Kennedy, whose veil was still down and still glistened with her tears as well. She took my hand and I said, 'I would like to express the personal sorrow of my family and of the people of Texas at your terrible loss.'

"Still holding my hand, she said, 'Please tell your mother that I am so glad your father is going to be all right. That's the only good thing that has come of this.'"

John then gave her his mother's note, and in that moment, a seventeen-year-old had grown up.

• • •

Back in Texas, Connally children Sharon and Mark finally got to see their recovering father a few days later when they traveled to Dallas and shared Thanksgiving dinner with him in his Parkland Hospital room.

There was no doubt about why they were thankful.

‖‖

CHAPTER TWELVE

GOVERNOR CONNALLY SPEAKS

It was the day after President Kennedy had been buried, and most of the Press Corps had faded away from Parkland Hospital. Charles Murphy of WBAP, the local NBC station, approached me and said that the assassination story would not be complete until the world could hear from Governor John Connally. He was, after all, the ultimate witness, having come close to death himself from one of the bullets that killed President Kennedy. Murphy urged that Connally speak to the media.

I understood his point. I earlier had reflected on the irony that, if at any other time, a Texas governor—or any governor—were to be critically wounded by gunfire, it would have been giant headline news. However, a United States president had been murdered and Connally's wounds, though critical and incurred at the president's side, understandably were a far subordinated story.

I weighed Murphy's request with real concern. The governor was only a few days removed from four hours of surgery. A gaping chest wound was barely closed, a useless right arm hung limply overhead, tubes still protruded from his body, and he was very weak.

Yes, I agreed to the importance that he be heard, but I could not subject him to a conventional news conference, given his still-tenuous condition.

The solution that I proposed to Governor Connally was to arrange an exclusive bedside interview by a single designated newsman. We would offer it live to the three major television networks of that time—ABC, CBS, and NBC—at 4:30 p.m. Dallas time, to be aired in full and without edits. It was a take-it-or-leave-it offering. As far as I knew, such conditions never had been imposed on a national broadcast news network, but I felt they were justified under the circumstances. Predictably, the proposed arrangements were not received without controversy. Dick Salant, president of CBS News, took serious issue in a telegram protesting the conditions. To his credit, however, Salant and officials at NBC and ABC ultimately accepted the arrangements in good faith.

My choice for the delicate and challenging assignment was Martin Agronsky, a highly respected NBC correspondent with whom we had worked in the past. Governor Connally agreed to the arrangements.

At our request, NBC located Agronsky at Arlington National Cemetery in Washington, where he was mourning the passing of the president. Agronsky later boarded a red-eye flight to Dallas, grabbing a few hours of sleep on arriving that morning. He then conducted the agreed-on fifteen-minute bedside interview with Governor Connally that aired simultaneously on all three national networks late that afternoon. The governor lucidly described the horror inside the presidential limousine before he lost consciousness as a result of his wounds.

Connally was well aware of the trauma and uncertainty being felt by citizens across the country in the wake of the Kennedy assassination. His comments during the interview regarding the new president were credited with helping give assurance to Americans who knew little of Lyndon Johnson, the man who now was their leader.

Connally said in part, "I know of no man I would rather have dealing my hand in this hour of tragedy."

John and Nellie Connally left Parkland Hospital and returned to Austin ten days after he was wounded by the same assassin who killed President John F. Kennedy as the two men were basking in the success of their motorcade through downtown Dallas.

Dr. Shaw and other dedicated staff members at Parkland had worked their medical magic by now, and thanks to their skills, the governor had survived a very close call. Beyond physical trauma, he experienced recurring nightmares in which a gunman always chased him.

During this time, however, he had ridden a wave of public concern and sympathy.

Even longtime political adversaries softened their view toward him. After he returned to the Governor's Mansion surrounded by a phalanx of state troopers, he enjoyed a season of good will. He was, for all intents and practical purposes, politically untouchable.

All of that did little to minimize the practical everyday consequences of the serious injuries he had incurred. His right arm would be in a sling for weeks—public pictures of which prompted well-wishers to send him a sizable collection of additional slings, even some styled for formal wear. For a period, his appearances approached the status of a reluctant celebrity.

In the meantime, legislative aide Temple recalls that Connally complained repeatedly about the frustration of trying to balance peas on the fork with his left hand. A more persistent challenge was that of having to sign official documents with his left hand. Over ensuing months, Connally's left-handed signatures became prized collectors' items.

Executive Assistant Howard Rose remembers that gubernatorial appointments became a tedious and dreaded chore for the governor as he struggled through rehabilitation.

Most people are not aware that the selection of qualified candidates for state governmental boards and commissions is not a favorite endeavor for governors, even in good times. It is conventional political wisdom that for every one person you make happy with an appointment, you make several more unhappy because they were not chosen.

"We already were behind on appointments," Rose said.

He recounted with a laugh the times that all of us rode down to the Connally's ranch southeast of San Antonio specifically to work on appointments, only to spend too much time driving with the governor around the ranch, as he procrastinated on selection of the nominees.

Even as Connally doggedly stuck to the task of appointments and many other responsibilities, all of us saw a deeper change in his demeanor. He had less patience with petty matters. Like many who have had a close brush with death, he became more reflective about life. I recall one ride with him across the countryside when he commented on the simple blessing of enjoying the beauty of trees and flowers around us, obviously expressing gratitude for life itself.

A few weeks into the governor's recovery, the Connallys were paid a visit during the Christmas holidays by longtime friends Lyndon and Lady Bird Johnson. Their relationship went back many years, including when Lady Bird and Nellie shared a small apartment in Washington while their husbands went off to the service in World War II. But now, the cosmic result of that day in Dallas was that LBJ was president of the United States and Lady Bird the first lady.

At that time, not even yet a teenager, Mark Connally still remembers that, as he had done many times before, he rushed up to Johnson and exclaimed "Hello, Uncle Lyndon."

"Dad admonished me," he said. "'Mark, you need to address him as "Mr. President" now.'"

Whereupon, President Johnson replied, "I am still Uncle Lyndon to you."

When the governor began his long recovery road, Nellie came back to the Mansion and recorded her own fresh memory of the horror she had lived since leaving there almost two weeks earlier.

She sat down with a yellow legal pad and pencil and wrote in longhand all that she had witnessed and felt throughout the ordeal. She did so not for any public purpose, she said. Instead, she was motivated by the thought that her potential grandchildren might someday want to know more about what happened to their grandfather and grandmother far back in history. Her task completed, Nellie placed her notes into a metal filing cabinet and forgot them for forty years.

CHAPTER THIRTEEN

||||||||||||||||||||||||||||||||||||||||||||||||||||||||||||||||||||||||||||||||||||||||||||||||||||||||||||||||||||||||||||||||||||||||

NELLIE'S FORGOTTEN NOTES

Those pages of Nellie Connally's handwritten notes remained forgotten until July 2002, when I accompanied her to an appearance on *Larry King Live* to discuss her harrowing experience of November 22, 1963.

Among the many viewers watching that night was prominent author and literary agent Bill Adler, an influential fixture in New York publishing circles for decades. Adler was intrigued by what he heard, and sensed a book in the making.

Nellie Connally was pleased to hear from Adler but was skeptical about the venture. She and I had spent several days in New York City a number of years earlier, exploring interest for her story. Six publishers had seen us, and while all were charmed by her and loved the visits, no book offers were forthcoming. This was at the beginning of tougher times in the publishing industry, and book deals were being made only on sure successes.

This time around things were different. Adler secured the interest of a fledgling young publisher in the South Houston Street (SoHo) neighborhood of New York, and a full-blown infatuation with the literary world ensued.

The publication of Nellie's book and its subsequent promotion proved to be a warm and gratifying experience that kindled a new spirit in Nellie at age eighty-three. After a lifetime of banking her vivacious persona and natural affinity for the stage to defer to her husband's career, it was now her time to take center stage and the spotlight in her own right.

With the help of Houston writer Mickey Herskowitz, who earlier had coauthored Governor Connally's book, Nellie completed the work with passion, expanding her commentary into greater detail from her notes. I assisted in the editing.

The book was published in 2003 and featured a cover photo of two happy, handsome couples—President and Mrs. Kennedy and John and Nellie Connally—smiling to adoring crowds in downtown Dallas.

My daughter Ellen Read and I, along with the publisher's publicist, helped orchestrate a national book tour, beginning with readings and signing parties in major Texas cities. It was highlighted by a star-studded gala reception in New York, where guests included Walter and Betsy Cronkite, Barbara Walters, and Brian Williams.

I always felt that the book journey not only gave Nellie her long-delayed stage appearance, but it also provided her a needed catharsis for all that she had absorbed many years before.

I know from personal experience that she never fully cleansed herself of the anguish that she carried as a result of that indescribable moment in the presidential limousine.

Like a parent proud that her children had been polite to company, she had been almost giddy over the warmth shown the president by Dallas when she turned to him to speak the last words he would ever hear: "Mr. President, you certainly can't say that Dallas doesn't love you." Seconds later, she almost lost her husband. But beyond her own nightmare, I heard her say on more than one occasion that she understood fully the bitterness that the Kennedy family might feel toward Texas and that she always felt so helpless to heal the hurt that they had suffered.

While she and Jacqueline Kennedy exchanged kind and touching messages following the assassination, Nellie went to her grave disappointed that she never was able to establish any real contact with the Kennedys' daughter, Caroline. At one point, she wrote Caroline a plaintive note expressing her long-held sorrow and her wish to establish a correspondence. She also added that she understood if Caroline chose not to do so.

No reply ever came. Nellie even went so far as to contact Caroline's office to confirm that her message had been received. She asked me what else, if anything, she should do. I advised her to let it go.

•   •   •

A melancholy footnote: When Mrs. Connally failed to answer the door at Austin's exclusive Westminster Manor retirement center the morning of September 1, 2006, authorities found her slumped body beside her writing desk.

On the desk was a partially finished thank-you note for my help on her book tour.

‖‖‖

CHAPTER FOURTEEN

DALLAS LEFT IN SHOCK AND SHAME

Much has been written about those dark hours and days following the nightmare in downtown Dallas. Along with the rest of the world, I watched in shock the televised scenes of Lyndon B. Johnson and Air Force One taking off from Love Field for Washington, D.C., carrying the body of the fallen president and his bereft widow.

But back in Texas, the wounded city of Dallas remained behind, drifting in a daze of shock, pain, and blame.

By the time flags fell to half-mast on the afternoon of the assassination, the air was already filling with bitterness and recrimination for the assassination of John F. Kennedy. The subsequent murder of Lee Harvey Oswald seared emotions even more intensely.

Many declared Dallas the "City of Hate" for the first crime. Its police department was derided as "Keystone Cops" for permitting the second.

There were quick, broad, and brutal expressions of anger. Dallas Mayor Earle Cabell received death threats and required police protection when he and San Antonio Mayor Walter McAllister attended the Kennedy funeral services in Washington, D.C. Texas Attorney General Waggoner Carr was forcefully pinned against the back of a hotel elevator by an antagonistic crowd when he represented Texas at the same events.

A prominent Dallas business leader was thrown out of a New York taxicab when the driver learned he was from Dallas.

Families traveling outside the state sometimes experienced reluctant, or even were denied, service in restaurants when it was learned they were from Dallas.

As further evidence of the fury toward Dallas, Southern Methodist University historian Darwin Payne points to a sheaf of letters in the school's DeGolyer Library attacking Cabell for the two murders. Payne covered the assassination as a young reporter for the *Dallas Times Herald*.

A current Dallas leader remembers that as a youngster, he and fellow Boy Scouts were warned in advance about reaction they might receive on an upcoming visit to Pennsylvania when people saw the Dallas patch on their uniforms.

Then twelve-year-old Robert Decherd, now chairman of Dallas's Belo Corporation, had a similar experience on a trip with his parents to England and Ireland.

"When they found out you were from Dallas, their entire expressions changed, and in clear indications . . . they let you know they didn't want to know you," he recalls.

A Dallas business owner dependent on direct-mail orders was forced to change her postal address to nearby Arlington, Texas, when her orders dropped 90 percent following the assassination.

Was Dallas a "City of Hate"? Sentiments were sharply divided. One local public official openly claimed that to be a fact. Others agreed with the popular Dallas high school cheerleader who sobbed and blurted out, "I hate Dallas. I'm ashamed to be a Texan."

In contrast, during her first public remarks following the tragedy, survivor and Texas First Lady Nellie Connally had pleaded to the public: "Please do not blame Dallas."

In the years that followed, anguished Dallasites pointed out that Los Angeles was not blamed for the assassination of Bobby Kennedy, nor was Memphis blamed for the death of Martin Luther King Jr.

Why then, was Dallas alone among cities held responsible for a heinous act that occurred within its boundaries?

The stinging charge against Dallas was fueled largely by the combination of interrelated influences, unfair as it might seem. To begin with, this was the first such assassination of the modern era. But just as importantly, the city's political climate at that time was characterized by a number of ultraconservative voices and forces that engaged in aggressive dialogue and actions.

The John Birch Society, considered by many to be conservatively extremist, was based in Dallas. An outspoken rightwinger, General Edwin E. Walker, had set up shop in Dallas. Oil man H. L. Hunt aired ultraconservative and somewhat radical views on a local radio program. Sitting Republican U.S. Congressman Bruce Alger was so conservative that he refused to support a community effort to build a new federal building and even went so far as to vote against free school lunches.

On November 4, 1960, Congressman Alger organized a protest rally against then–Senate Majority Leader Lyndon B. Johnson as Johnson campaigned for vice president on the ticket with John F. Kennedy. In the course of that rally, Lady Bird Johnson was reported to have been spat at.

Three years later, on October 24, 1963, just weeks before the Kennedys came to Dallas, a group of right-wing extremists disrupted a speech by United Nations Ambassador Adlai Stevenson at the city's Memorial Auditorium Theater. In the ensuing frenzy, one woman struck Stevenson with a sign. The well-known right-winger General Edwin Walker had delivered a fiery speech at a rally the night before that was credited with inciting followers to infiltrate and disrupt the ambassador's appearance the next day.

The following week, *Time* magazine reported on the incident under the headline: "Dallas: A City Disgraced."

Finally, there was the unfortunate full-page newspaper advertisement, bordered in black, that greeted President Kennedy the morning he came to Dallas, after handbills were circulated calling for his impeachment.

In his oral history at the Sixth Floor Museum, the late *Dallas Morning News* publisher Joe Dealey laments that he probably would not have allowed publication of the advertisement if he had been in the city at the time and had known about it.

All of these factors rightfully or wrongfully contributed to largely negative perceptions of the city. As the hate charges mounted, bitter debate ensued, with ample passion and rhetoric on both sides.

Dallas School Superintendent W. T. White suspended a teacher for writing a letter to a newspaper blaming the city. A firestorm erupted against him. In a Sixth Floor Museum oral history from almost three decades later, former Mayor Jonsson protests plaintively: "I don't hate anyone."

Thus began a long and tortuous road to the rehabilitation of the reputation and recovery of spirit of a great American city.

The Fort Worth Star-Telegram *announced the president's death with the first Extra edition it had published since 1949.*

Shock and confusion outside the emergency entrance at Parkland Hospital.

Two thousand four hundred unsuspecting luncheon guests awaiting the president's arrival at the Trade Mart in Dallas.

Empty, silent auditorium in Austin tells its own story.

A prayer service at the Capitol replaces the gala celebration.

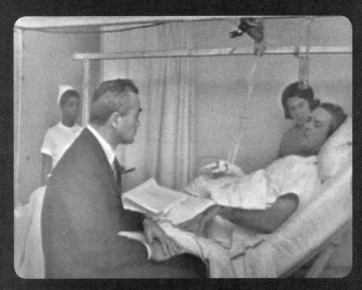

(top) Nellie Connally speaks to the press at Parkland Hospital.

(bottom) Texas Governor John Connally being interviewed by newsman Martin Agronsky at bedside in Parkland Hospital.

B41N
URGENT
1ST NIGHT LEAD CONNALLY (B30) CD/
BY KYLE THOMPSON
UNITED PRESS INTERNATIONAL
DALLAS, NOV. 24 (UPI)--TEXAS GOV. JOHN CONNALLY, GRAVELY WOUNDED
DURING THE ASSASSINATION OF PRESIDENT KENNEDY LAT FRIDAY, FELT SO
GOOD TODAY HE WALKED FROM HIS BED TO A CHAIR AND SAT UP.
CONNALLY STAYED IN THE CHAIR A FEW MINUTES AND WALKED BACK TO BED,
SMILING.
HIS WIFE, NELLIE, WAS COMPOSED AS SHE TOLD NEWSMEN EARLIER IN THE
DAY THAT HER HUSBAND "IS NOW APPARENTLY OUT OF DANGER," BUT BROKE
INTO SOBS WHEN SHE SPOKE OF PRESIDENT KENNEDY.
(PICKUP 2, $ PGH: MRS. CONNALLY HELD)
                                                    K05 29 PES

CLASS OF SERVICE
This is a fast message
unless its deferred char-
acter is indicated by the
proper symbol.

WESTERN UNION
TELEGRAM
W. P. MARSHALL, PRESIDENT

SF-1201 (4-60)

SYMBOLS
DL=Day Letter
NL=Night Letter
LT=International
      Letter Telegram

The filing time shown in the date line on domestic telegrams is LOCAL TIME at point of origin. Time of receipt is LOCAL TIME at point of destination

206P CST NOV 27 63 DB207
D D CDV038 PD
TD CO NEW YORK NS 27 251P EST
JULIAN REED, EXECUTIVE ASST TO THE GOVERNOR OF TEXAS
    PARKLAND HOSPITAL DAL
WISH FORMERLY TO RECORD THE MOST VIGOROUS PROTEST OF CBS NEWS
TO THE SEVERAL CONDITIONS OF INTEVIEW SCHEDULED BY YOUR OFFICE
FOR THIS AFTERNOON. PARTICULARLY WE PROTEST 1 YOUR OFFICE'S
DESIGNATION OF WHO IS TO CONDUCT THE INTERVIEW 2 YOUR ASSUMING
THE RIGHT TO SELECT THE QUESTIONS TO BE PUT AND 3 THE IMPOSITION
OF THE CONDITION THAT THE ENTIRE INTERVIEW BE CARRIED IN FULL
    WITHOUT THE RIGHT OF THE NEWS MEDIA TO SELECT IT OR COMPRESS.
THESE ARE CONDITIONS TOTALLY CONTRARY TO SOUND JOURNALISTIC
PRACTICE AND PRECEDENT AND I URGE YOU TO RECONSIDER
    RICHARD SALANT PRESIDENT CBS NEWS 485 MADISON AVE NEW YORK
NY

*A wire report and a telegram from the author's
makeshift desk at Parkland Hospital.*

Howard Rose

1. Hands off public next few days
   Shift again to medical/medical week?

Make announcement to Board of Control

2.

3. Rep to Gov's funeral? State Holiday?

4. Joint Session of House + Senate / man present

Condition /
2. Mrs. Connally
   How government run?

3. When up and about?
   10-14

— had a very close call

Condition improved

NBC = 4 mins

what sort of arrangement

Condition

Mrs. ... Noble

Mother, brothers + sisters
no other visitors

Progress still satisfactory

Sat on side of bed
with help

no longer critical

Glimpses of Read's scrawled notes following the tragedy. Saved by his assistant, the notes and papers from the immediate aftermath of the assassination were sent to Read thirty-five years later.

Draft of Texas Governor Connally's telegram to Jacqueline Kennedy.

The Connallys' elder son, John, represented the family at the Kennedy funeral ceremonies in Washington, D.C.

(above) The Johnsons and Connallys are reunited at the Texas Governor's Mansion during the Christmas holidays in 1963.

(opposite page) Julian Read helped coordinate Nellie Connally's national book tour.

WHAT'S RIGHT WITH DALLAS?

There has been a great deal of discussion about Dallas in recent weeks in both the domestic and foreign press. Some reporters have done a "quickie" on our city and others have stayed long enough to make less superficial studies. The truth of the matter is that no one can get to know a city in a day, a week, or a month. Those of us who have lived here for a lifetime are so close to the picture that we too sometimes fail to see either some of the pertinent details or the entire composition.

We think there's a lot right with Dallas. We think the dynamic growth of this city in the past thirty years has been no accident; that the factors that motivated this growth are still present and can continue to contribute to the development of Dallas as one of the major centers of distribution, banking, specialized manufacturing, insurance in the country. We think Dallas' leadership which has devoted itself unselfishly to community problems and needs is unique in the country. We think that our local government has been distinguished among all American cities by the integrity and honesty of its elected and appointed officials. We think that our citizens are friendly and kind hearted human beings who extend genuinely warm welcomes to newcomers to our city.

All of this doesn't mean that there aren't things about Dallas that couldn't be improved. As Erik Jonsson, our distinguished fellow citizen, said recently, "I have always believed that individuals, corporations, and communities should have a regular stock taking of what they are and what they are trying to be, and how they would accomplish their objectives. I do agree that this is a good time to do that stock taking. It is year end and this is traditionally a time of reflection and introspection." We concur with Mr. Jonsson that a city, like individuals or business institutions, must take an honest look at its inventory and be willing to consider its faults as well as its assets. A city like the individual or corporation can't stand still—it must go ahead or fall behind.

Here seems to us to be some of the areas for community improvement—areas in which each of us as citizens, taxpayers and voters can exercise both individual and collective influence. One, Dallas has a slum problem that it hasn't faced up to as yet. We've talked about it for years and we've done relatively little to improve blighted areas which won't disappear by wishful thinking. We have not solved the problem of low cost housing. Two, this community has suffered from a spirit of "absolutism" in

recent years. This was expressed most cogently in a recent editorial of the St. Louis Post-Dispatch:

"What should concern Dallas and every other city is that the extremists of far right and far left have this in common, that they alienate themselves from the main stream of American democracy by an absolutism of political temper which is fundamentally hostile to our principles."

"It is the absolutist, whether of left or right, that democracy has to fear. This is the man who thinks that he alone possesses wisdom, patriotism and virtue, who recognizes no obligation to accept community decisions with which he disagrees, who regards any means as justified by the end, who views the political process as a power struggle to impose conformity rather than a means of reconciling differences.

"Democracy is a method of reaching a consensus. Those who reject the consensus reject democracy."

The rejection of this spirit of "absolutism" and the acceptance and insistence by all citizens on toleration of differing points of view seem to us to be essential for the future health of our community. We believe our newspapers have an important contribution to make in regard to this matter and we hope they will lead the way by the presentation of balanced points of view on controversial issues.

Third, we are still a young city and much of our time and energy has been devoted to physical growth which has been phenomenal. Now, the time has come when more attention needs to be paid to the quality of our endeavors than the size of them. This applies to our schools and colleges, our symphonies, operas, and museums. It applies to the quality of support that we as citizens give them as well.

Finally, we think that Dallas should forget about its "civic image" as such. The best public relations comes from doing good things and by not doing bad things. Let's have more "fair play" for legitimate differences of opinion, less coverup for our obvious deficiences, less boasting about our attainments, more moral indignation by all of us when we see human rights imposed upon. Then we won't have to worry about the "Dallas Image"—it will take care of itself.

HAPPY NEW YEAR

Prominent community leader Erik Jonsson,
drafted to become mayor of Dallas in 1964.

*Dallas's first gesture to recognize the assassination, a stark
cenotaph erected in 1970 near the site of the tragedy.*

(above) The Dallas Morning News *credited Dallas County engineer Judson Shook, left of plaque, with "saving [the Texas School Book Depository] building from the wrecking ball."*

(below) Acclaimed Dallas preservationist Lindalyn Adams devoted thirteen years of her life to help make the Sixth Floor Museum a reality.

(*above*) *Dallas County Judge Lee Jackson joined earlier Judges Gary Weber, Frank Crowley, and Dave Fox to purchase and renovate the Depository building and to help create the Sixth Floor Museum.*

(*below*) *Conover Hunt, left, with Adams, combined skills with perseverance to overcome obstacles and complete the museum.*

*The proud Dealey family name became forever
linked with the Kennedy tragedy.*

Curious visitors from around the world
appear on the plaza at all hours.

The Investigations

The Sixth Floor Museum is open daily except Thanksgiving and Christmas Day.

*Thousands of young students learn about
the assassination at the museum.*

President Johnson signs the Voting Rights Act in 1965.

President Johnson and civil rights leader Martin Luther King Jr. celebrate passage of the Voting Rights Act.

"We celebrate the past to awaken the future."
John F. Kennedy, 1960

Fort Worth's JFK Tribute plaza, where Kennedy spoke to a large crowd on the morning of November 22. It was created under the leadership of Downtown Fort Worth, Inc., and preservationists/philanthropists Shirlee and Taylor Gandy.

CHAPTER FIFTEEN

||||||||||||||||||||||||||||||||||||||||||||||||||||||||||||||||||||||||||||||||||||||||||||||||||||||||||||||||||||||||

FIRST STEPS
TOWARD RECOVERY

While Dallas leaders worked to shape a plan toward recovery in the months that followed, the city remained in shock, distress, and paralysis in the wake of the assassination.

Most residents wished to simply forget the tragedy as if it had been some bad dream. Certainly there was no interest—except among historians—in memorializing the event. In fact, Dallas was so eager to put the tragedy behind it that as former Mayor Wes Wise recalls, the city's influential Press Club chose not to include a single mention of the tragedy in its 1964 Gridiron Show, an event that usually focuses on highlights of the past year.

"We just wanted to get away from the nightmare," Wise said.

Meanwhile, continuing streams of visitors from around the world collected and milled around the notorious Texas School Book Depository building every day, incessantly peering up toward its sixth floor window, where Kennedy's assassin had hidden amid a stack of boxes.

Half a block away from the crime scene, up Elm Street, an enterprising businessman opened a modest storefront souvenir shop. While many cringed at the crass commercialization of the tragedy, the City of Dallas did nothing to acknowledge or memorialize the episode with an act of official recognition.

There had been some encouraging developments toward healing, however.

Globally known Dallas merchant Stanley Marcus, who had advised President Kennedy against coming to Dallas out of concern for his safety, gave the community a much-needed infusion of spirit with a full-page newspaper ad asking, "What's Right With Dallas?"

On the political front, Dallas Mayor Earle Cabell challenged right-wing leader Bruce Alger for his seat in Congress in the 1964 election. Cabell had the backing of the establishment community, which was eager to moderate the city's extremist image as epitomized by Alger. As Cabell left the post of mayor to make the race, community titan Erik Jonsson, who had worked tirelessly to respond to the tragedy, was drafted by city leaders to succeed Cabell in that office. It was one of the most important developments in the recovery period. As head of the powerful Citizens Council, Jonsson was highly regarded as a strong and effective leader. He also had felt firsthand the anguish of November 22 as chairman of the ill-fated Trade Mart luncheon.

Jonsson recounts in his oral history that he initially turned down the draft to succeed Cabell as mayor. Undeterred, friends turned to his wife, Margaret, to plead their case. She called her husband afterward and told him he should take the job. Jonsson admits that his final decision was influenced by his despair over the stains that continued to soil his beloved city. Cabell defeated Alger handily for the seat in Congress in November of 1964, the same year that Lyndon Johnson swept to victory for a full term as president. The aggressive right-wing voices began to recede in the Dallas community.

Newly elected Mayor Jonsson undertook decisive leadership initiatives and fashioned an ambitious "Goals for Dallas" plan designed to put the city on a positive track with a number of bold initiatives, including design and construction of a new City Hall. Pierce Allman, then news director for WFAA radio, said that Jonsson's efforts to bring the city's disparate elements together to identify and address community problems such as race relations "had an enormous healing effect." (Allman certainly had an informed perspective of that time. He had given the first radio report of the shooting from a phone inside the lobby of the Texas School Book Depository. He was directed to that phone by a young man rushing out the front door, who later was identified to have been Lee Harvey Oswald.) Another important development came when, after years of sibling standoff between Dallas and Fort Worth, Jonsson went to work with Fort Worth Mayor Bayard Friedman to move forward on building a gigantic new joint airport, larger than the island of Manhattan. It would prove to be a remarkable economic development engine that brought monumental growth and benefits to the Dallas–Fort Worth area.

John and Nellie Connally testified before the Warren Commission in April 1964. That body issued its report late that year finding that Lee Harvey Oswald was the lone assassin of President Kennedy.

And every November nearing the assassination anniversary date, starting in 1964, I would coordinate countless media requests for Governor Connally to recite memories of his awful near-death experience in the streets of Dallas. However, it would be years before the city itself would come to terms with the fate it had been dealt. Indeed, it was not until 1970 that the first step came, when prominent architect Philip Johnson was commissioned by Dallas citizens, following his selection by the Kennedy family, to design a memorial to commemorate the president's death. Notwithstanding the stature of the creative artist, the result that rose on a nearby city square turned out to be a somewhat austere, if not sterile, concrete box structure—a cenotaph, or open tomb. The controversial effort was judged by many to be inappropriate or insufficient for its purpose. One noted architectural critic said that the president "deserved better." Interestingly, community donors to that project declined to have their names publicly disclosed, reflecting the sensitivity of that time.

More meaningful steps to recognize and memorialize the assassination would not come for almost a decade.

CHAPTER SIXTEEN

||||||||||||||||||||||||||||||||||||||||||||||||||||||||||||||||||||||||||||||||||||||||||||||||||||||||||||||

SAVIOR OF THE SCHOOL BOOK DEPOSITORY

The hordes of visitors who stream through today's Sixth Floor Museum are indebted to a now-deceased Dallas County engineer named C. Judson Shook Jr., a graduate of the U.S. Naval Academy and retired colonel in the Air Force, for their experience. Without his vision and quiet will, the building in which the Texas School Book Depository was housed very likely would have been destroyed. In Shook's 2010 obituary the *Dallas Morning News* credited him with "saving [the Depository] from the wrecking ball."

As most Dallasites struggled to insulate or remove themselves from the tragedy that had left a disfiguring mark on their city, the one who perhaps had the most trouble doing that was Shook, who became director of public works for the county in 1968.

The window of Shook's public works office was directly across the street from the notorious building. Through his window there was a direct view of incessant crowds of the curious who gathered below and then milled around on the street in front of it and the adjacent Dealey Plaza. From the time Shook first occupied his office in 1977, he observed daily the endless streams of visitors craning their necks for a glance upward to the sixth-floor window, where Kennedy's assassin had lurked.

Over months of observing that scene below, Shook gradually became convinced that the structure should be saved because of its historical significance, regardless of any individual's viewpoint of the tragedy or of the city's interest in forgetting it even happened.

The building had experienced a troubled history since the Kennedy assassination in November 1963. Its major tenant vacated its space in 1970. A Tennessee entrepreneur purchased the warehouse from owner Colonel D. H. Byrd with the intent to establish a Kennedy museum there. But ownership reverted to Byrd after a failed arson attempt and default on the purchaser's loan.

During the time that the structure sat unoccupied and deteriorating, Dallas County had developed a growing need for additional space in which to consolidate its broadening range of functions. Shook found himself in the position to reconcile two needs in one strategic action. In an oral history at today's Sixth Floor Museum, he observes that while he considered other sites for the county offices, he clearly preferred the depository building, not only because of its historical significance but also because of the structural quality of the building.

Shook clearly saw the opportunity for a double win. He could acquire much-needed additional space for the county and perhaps also make available some of the floor space for the creation of a historical memorial to the tragedy that occurred there.

Shook knew that many still held the view that the building should be bulldozed to remove a bitter and visible reminder of the tragedy. Indeed, former Dallas Mayor Wes Wise described in an interview how he once had stepped in to block a motion before the Dallas City Council to do just that.

Aware of the political sensitivities for elected members of the Dallas County Commissioners Court, Shook personally undertook presenting the initiative to the public. Thanks to his credibility and willingness to take the heat, only scattered opposition surfaced. The purchase of the building was authorized by decisive voter approval as part of a 1977 bond issue. Dallas County acquired the property in 1978 for a new Commissioners Court courtroom and administrative offices.

After voters approved purchase of the building, Shook wanted to test his idea with the historical preservation community. So he called Lindalyn Adams, chairman of the Dallas County Historical Commission, to set up an exploratory meeting.

"Now that we own this building, we need to know what to do with that floor—what to do with the sixth floor," he said in that March 1977 meeting in which he asked for her help. Adams describes her initial shock on hearing his concept in her oral history at today's Sixth Floor Museum. But she continued to listen.

Beyond having the vision and passion to save the building, Shook personally oversaw its journey to adaptive reuse in the best historical preservation tradition. Impressed by the earlier restoration of Dallas's historic downtown Cumberland School building to become headquarters for former Texas Governor Bill Clements's SEDCO drilling company, Shook sought out its architect, Rodger Burson, and engaged him to restore and adapt the building for the county's use.

Throughout that process, Shook displayed a sensitivity approaching paternal stewardship of the building as it was reshaped around an imposing two-story atrium that today houses the Commissioners Court itself. With a keen eye to historic features, he even insisted on moving an original pressed metal ceiling to a lower floor for public viewing.

Dallas County moved into the former Texas School Book Depository building in 1978, and it was dedicated on March 29, 1981 as the Dallas County Administration Building. While the first five floors were rehabilitated and occupied in phases, the top two floors remained empty and unchanged, including the haunting sixth floor corner.

Shook was quoted in a 1978 *Dallas Morning News* article as saying that the space would remain vacant until "history decides what to do with it."

What would happen to that space ultimately came to depend on Lindalyn Adams and her preservation allies. Her life would not be the same for the next thirteen years. But the history of November 22, 1963, finally had the hope for a suitable home.

||||||||||||||||||||||||||||||||||||||||||||||||||||||||||||||||||||||||||||||||||||||||||||||||||||||||||||||||||||||

CHAPTER SEVENTEEN

PATRON SAINT OF THE SIXTH FLOOR MUSEUM

Today's Sixth Floor Museum in downtown Dallas is both the emblematic and substantive soul of the city's recovery from the dark days of 1963, and community culture guardian Lindalyn Adams was its patron saint through the long journey from concept to realization.

Adams had already earned her pedigree in historic preservation before Judson Shook came calling about the Texas School Book Depository building after he succeeded in purchasing it to house the county's Commissioners Court and administrative offices.

As far back as her year as a young provisional in the Junior League, Adams served as a docent at Fair Park's historic Hall of State. As president of the Dallas County Heritage Commission in 1972, she worked on efforts to preserve Old City Park and from 1975 had served as chairman of the Dallas County Historical Society. A force to be reckoned with, she was described by one official as "a Mack truck inside a powder puff."

Moreover, she and husband Reuben, a prominent physician and leader at Baylor Hospital and medical school, were both respected community figures, long-rooted in exclusive Highland Park, the close-in enclave of Dallas's leading and most publicly active citizens.

That said, she was hardly a central casting choice to lead a project to memorialize the assassination of a Democratic president. Like most of her Junior League friends, she was a Republican and had not voted for President Kennedy. She definitely had not attended the aborted nonpartisan luncheon to honor him at the Dallas Trade Mart.

She even admitted ruefully in a 1997 Sixth Floor Museum oral history that in the fall of 1960, while handing out leaflets for Congressman Bruce Alger at the Adolphus Hotel with some of her friends, she found herself inadvertently caught up around the crowd that was to disrupt the appearance there of Lyndon and Lady Bird Johnson. She became alarmed at the tone of the demonstration and quickly left the scene.

So when Shook called and told her in March 1977 that he wanted her guidance to help establish an historical exhibit about the assassination on the sixth floor of the Texas School Book Depository, her response was an incredulous, "You want to do what?"

As a lifelong Dallas community leader stung by recriminations that had marred the image of her beloved city, Adams shared the inclination of most residents who wanted to forget the assassination—to put it behind them. She still recalls an occasion during a trip to the Caribbean in 1989, twenty-six years after the tragedy, when a woman, a stranger, after learning where she was from, observed, "That's where you kill presidents."

Still, aware of her position as a preservation leader and as a courtesy to Shook, Adams agreed to meet and to accompany him and film producer Martin Jurow to the still-vacant and untouched sixth floor, where assassin Lee Harvey Oswald had hidden among shipping boxes fourteen years before.

Reluctant as she was to go, Adams experienced an unexpected epiphany. In a later interview, she recalled solemnly how her attitude changed as she rode with Shook up the musty freight elevator amid spooky shadows and made her way to the solitary corner window where Oswald had waited patiently for his opportunity to fire on the slowly moving motorcade below.

"It was eerie," she said. "I was particularly struck by how close that window was to the street down below. I never have hunted in my life, but I believe even I could have shot [and hit] someone from there."

From that stark and revelatory moment, Lindalyn Adams was on board emotionally for what was to be a turbulent thirteen-year ride leading efforts that would ultimately result in the realization of today's respected and popular Sixth Floor Museum at Dealey Plaza. From that first meeting, Adams always felt comfortable working with Shook, she said.

As previously noted, on Judson Shook's recommendation, Dallas County purchased the Texas School Book Depository building in 1977 as part of a bond issue and began renovation of lower floors to become its Commissioners Court and administrative offices. However, the sixth floor was sealed off and remained in its original condition.

Adams's long and tedious journey began in early 1978. She began talking up the project in her circle of preservationists. She remembers seeing the inevitable and uniform shock on the faces of her colleagues. Nevertheless, despite some reservations, she gradually began to gain the faith and pledges of support from her own historical society and allied organizations. One of her most important initial breaks was an introduction, through a preservation colleague, to Conover Hunt, a talented and fearless young woman with strong academic and professional credentials in historic preservation.

Hunt, who with her husband had moved to Dallas from Virginia, suggested that the society submit a grant request to the National Endowment for the Humanities (NEH) to fund the convening of a planning panel of experts, a move that could open other doors to project funding. Convinced that "this woman knows what she is talking about," Adams moved to gather resolutions from state groups in her network of contacts to support the application. In January 1979, the project received a $15,000 grant matched by work of that value provided by the county to produce a tentative plan that was focused on conceptualization and feasibility.

The panel was assembled for a two-day meeting in April 1979 and included some of the state's most prominent preservation and architectural experts. Additional consultation took place with Texas Historical Commission Executive Director Truett Latimer at the State Capitol. And with Conover Hunt acting as facilitator, the panel wrote a report that years later produced a finished product remarkably faithful to the initial concept, according to Adams.

But the realization of that solid concept was to be a long journey, which was just beginning.

CHAPTER EIGHTEEN

||||||||||||||||||||||||||||||||||||||||||||||||||||||||||||||||||||||||||||||||||||||||||||||||||||||||||||||||||||||||||||||

UPS AND DOWNS TO REACH THE GOAL

As auspicious as the planning exercise had been, the initial museum effort was followed by a series of challenges and setbacks that spanned years. It was only Adams and her team's doggedness and patience, aided by timely and unexpected help along the way, that enabled eventual success.

Adams, Shook, and architect Rodger Burson encountered a dismissive attitude when they traveled to Washington in 1979 for a meeting with the National Park Service to seek placement of the building on the National Register of Historic Places.

Prior to their appointment, at a nearby restaurant, the three representatives happened to be seated close enough to agency officials to overhear staff members mocking their mission.

"Next, they'll want to put Watergate on the National Register!" one said.

In the meeting that followed, however, the staff actually warmed up to the proposal after seeing the NEH study that Adams had brought along. Even so, no assistance was to materialize from that source until years later.

Adams and her cohorts had managed to assemble some $200,000 in seed money, but half of that disappeared when the largest donor withdrew a $100,000 grant. The chairman of the leading Dallas foundation that had pledged the funding was vacillating as to the appropriateness of the project. Fortunately, that grant was later restored and ultimately increased through the tireless effort of a member of the same foundation's board.

Things truly began to look up after Dallas County completed rehabilitation of the former Texas School Book Depository and dedicated it as its new administration building on March 29, 1981.

Led by County Judge Gary Weber and Commissioner Roy Orr, the Commissioners Court appropriated $66,000 to pay for the development of conceptual plans for the Sixth Floor Museum. That funding enabled the project to bring in the nationally known design firm Staples & Charles to undertake that task. The plans developed as a consequence of that pivotal decision proved to be a key asset in establishing the project's credibility and would help to weather further fund-raising setbacks that loomed ahead. It was Barbara Staples who named the exhibit The Sixth Floor Museum.

In 1981, John Hinckley shot President Ronald Reagan outside a Washington, D.C., hotel. Hinckley was a former Dallas resident, and his background reopened old emotional wounds from 1963, throwing a damper on interest in financial support of the sixth floor project. Thus began a period when progress in the development slowed.

Starting in 1982, guiding spirit Adams was herself

slowed, as she was forced to deal with breast cancer. She was to face a first and then a second surgery. During the same time, dynamic project director Conover Hunt was temporarily called back to her home state, Virginia, and yet another staff member left to have a baby.

The project was forced to consider outsourcing its development efforts.

At one point, a New York fund-raiser with big promises was engaged using part of the project's modest nest egg to approach national foundations for contributions. That effort failed to raise a single cent. Financial support would henceforth have to come from home base.

In 1983, the Dallas Historical Foundation was formed to create a legal nonprofit entity that could accept financial contributions to benefit the Sixth Floor Museum and other projects. Until this time, the project had operated under the aegis of the Dallas Historical Commission. Lindalyn Adams was named chairman of the foundation, a post she had held earlier on the Historical Commission by appointment of the Commissioners Court.

The Historical Foundation elected a board of prominent citizens, including Shirley Caldwell, William Collins, William Cooper, Joe Dealey Sr., Jess Hay, Boone Powell Sr., Sam Moreno, Major General Hugh Robinson, Harriet Weber, Becky Power, John Crain, and Tom Smith.

That year, 1983, was the twentieth anniversary of the assassination of President Kennedy in Dallas, and Adams remembers a flood of media calls and public dialogue, ranging from "Why is it taking Dallas so long to do something like this [the museum]?" to "Why in the world would you want to do something like this?"

For several years to follow, the project struggled against still-divided emotions and apathy.

On December 30, 1986, Adams received an unexpected call that galvanized support and put the project on a trajectory toward successful completion.

The caller was Richard Sellers of the U.S. Department of the Interior, the National Park Service, based in Santa Fe, New Mexico. He had heard of the Texas School Book Depository and was interested in paying a visit to the actual location. After touring the site and studying the plan for development, Sellers told Adams, "This more than meets the standards of the National Park Service" and said that his office would be available to help.

Two days later, Adams got another welcome surprise.

In his inaugural remarks, newly elected Dallas County Judge Lee Jackson announced that one of his goals was to complete the Sixth Floor Museum.

"It was just like Christmas and New Year's all wrapped into one," Adams exclaimed.

While waiting to assume office after his election, Jackson had watched an endless flow of visitors coming to the court building entrance to ask how to get to the sixth floor.

"I knew we had to complete the project," he said in an interview. "I'm just glad that I was in a position to help."

Adams was elated. She immediately sought out Jackson and discussed how they might work together. Jackson joined three previous county judges—Gary Weber, Frank Crowley, and Dave Fox—in support of the project.

Buoyed by her sudden double serving of good fortune, Adams called all of her team members back together for a summit meeting to renew their long-standing efforts in order to complete the project while the upwardly trending support persisted.

Still more good news followed: project director Conover Hunt returned from Virginia, rejoining the efforts. On

March 23, 1987, the reorganized group assembled an unprecedented force of local, state, and federal officials in support of the exhibit. The list included Judge Jackson and other Dallas County Court officials, Richard Sellers and a delegation of National Park Service personnel, design experts Barbara Charles and Robert Staples, and other previously engaged consultants.

With new momentum established, Adams and her team, including board members and other volunteers, intensified their fund-raising efforts. Such community heavyweights as "Mr. Republican" Dave Fox and "Mr. Democrat" Jess Hay teamed up to host a series of fund-raising luncheons to motivate support.

Conover Hunt remembered making more than one hundred personal visits in the heat of a stifling Dallas summer. The fund-raisers made a point of paying priority calls—carrying with them a scale model of the exhibit—on prominent city leaders such as Mayor Erik Jonsson, Stanley Marcus, and John Stemmons. Adams especially remembers her emotional visit with Stemmons, a giant among community leaders. As a cochairman of the ill-fated Dallas Trade Mart luncheon on November 22, 1963, which President Kennedy never reached, Stemmons still bore the emotional wounds of that heartbreaking day.

Friends were so concerned for his despair that they feared he might consider suicide, given how deep the effect of the event was on him. After a long silence following Adams's presentation, Stemmons quietly said, "Well, let's go ahead. It's something we have to do."

Not all calls met with such support, due to some still-searing memories and conflicted feelings. For example, there was the well-known leader of one of the city's richest foundations, who was approached for participation.

"I can't contribute to that," he said, still remembering being thrown out of a New York taxicab because he was from Dallas.

However, real support finally was growing; there was a palpable momentum. A Sixth Floor Museum would soon be within reach.

|||||||||||||||||||||||||||||||||||||||||||||||||||||||||||||||||||||||||||||||||||||||||||||||||||||||||||||

CHAPTER NINETEEN

PROJECT "HEAVY" OVERCOMES CHALLENGES

As director of the project, Conover Hunt, the driven preservationist Texan transplant from Virginia, provided the professional glue to patch and hold together the planning and execution of the Sixth Floor Museum through years of stops and starts.

"She was absolutely wonderful in leading us through all of the challenges," said the project's guiding force, Lindalyn Adams. "Conover's combination of preservation skills and her hard-driving commitment was awesome."

Hunt knew a lot about the ins and outs of the preservation world from her studies at Tulane's Newcomb College and through the Winterthur Museum Program at the University of Delaware. She planned and led research and organizational projects with energy and sure-handedness.

Still, her knowledge and strong-headed will could not enable her to foresee all of the hurdles she would encounter as the ramrod of this endeavor.

Years later, Hunt could chuckle while recording her oral history at the Sixth Floor Museum as she recalled some of the roadblocks that she and her colleagues faced and overcame. None of them were foreseen in the original game plan.

For example, in the spring of 1987, Hunt was appalled to learn that the local Dallas Area Rapid Transit, known as DART, had decided to run its new light-rail system route through the assassination site. She spent long and determined hours fighting the plan, and her persistence paid off with an alternate route for the DART system at an acceptable distance away from the historic site.

Then, conflict arose between key preservation activists themselves regarding the proposed construction of a new passenger elevator attached to the rear of the building, a facility deemed critical to accommodate groups of visitors to the sixth floor.

Since the structure was within the West End Historic District of the city, any such plans were subject to approval of a local Landmark Task Force, which already had agreed in principle to the concept for the elevator as far back as 1983.

Now, new objections arose from a staff member of the task force, mainly over a sky bridge to connect the elevator to the rear of the building. To make matters worse, the Texas Historical Commission, the official state agency for preservation, joined in the opposition. However, the National Park Service, a strong new ally, supported the overall aims of the project. After what Adams and Hunt remember as a painful standoff between traditional allies, all parties finally came together at a meeting in the county's administration building to resolve their differences. Following further discussion, the task force ultimately approved the plan after some alteration to the length of the sky bridge.

One of Hunt's proudest achievements was the selection

of the widely renowned film team of Allen and Cynthia Mondell, with Hollywood producer Martin Jurow as an advisor, to produce a film centerpiece for the Sixth Floor Museum exhibit, with the script for the presentation written by Conover Hunt herself. The result was an award-winner after the film masters' artistry joined with the authoritative narration of Walter Cronkite, who donated his services in response to a request from his persuasive friend, Ambassador Robert Strauss.

There were other situations that Hunt could have done without.

For one, she can recall the day that the exterior brick that was to enclose all of the visitor center arrived on the scene. It was the wrong color. The error was corrected.

Then there was the timing of an ice storm that descended on Dallas just before the opening, while a large hole still gaped in the back of the sixth floor, and there still were no window panes in the visitor center. Meanwhile, a shipment of commemorative stamps for the gift shop remained inside an airplane, frozen like a popsicle in the ice of International Falls, Minnesota, one of the coldest spots in the country.

But in spite of obstacles and handicaps, the museum was opened to the public on Presidents' Day, February 20, 1989, to larger-than-expected crowds and decisive public approval.

A few years later, Hunt had another small surprise to overcome.

Now an independent consultant, she undertook the task of seeking National Historic Landmark status for Dealey Plaza, site of the assassination. The job was complicated by the fact the fifteen-acre site involved seven separate owners with whom to negotiate. However, the biggest last-minute challenge occurred just a few days before the scheduled designation ceremony. Hunt was aghast when she opened a package holding the bronze plate to be imbedded in the plaza and found that the name "Dealey" had been misspelled by the fabricator.

No problem for Hunt. When former Texas First Lady Nellie Connally delivered dedication remarks on November 22, 1993, the Dealey Plaza National Historic Landmark plaque contained no errors of spelling.

Hunt referred to herself as Lindalyn Adams's "heavy."

Adams called Hunt her "savior."

||||||||||||||||||||||||||||||||||||||||||||||||||||||||||||||||||||||||||||||||||||||||||||||||||||||||||

CHAPTER TWENTY

THE DALLAS MORNING NEWS *AND DEALEY PLAZA*

Much has been written and debated over whether the full-page ad attacking President Kennedy that appeared in the *Dallas Morning News* the morning of his arrival could have encouraged the assassination, although most feel that it later became obvious that Oswald had planned his action well before the ad was published.

Nevertheless, then-publisher of the *News* Joe Dealey states in his oral history at the Sixth Floor Museum that he believes he would have declined the ad had he been in town at the time it was submitted.

In the years after the assassination, regardless of conflicting views on that issue, there is no denying that Dealey was at the head of the line to help Dallas emerge from the stigma brought on by the killings. He was among the first to step forward to assist Lindalyn Adams in her quest to create the Sixth Floor Museum, both as an earlier member of the Dallas Historical Society and later as a foundation board member and major financial contributor. He was ultimately responsible for donations from the *News* and radio station WFAA that constituted nearly half of the $200,000-plus raised in the early years of the endeavor. Additional fundraising efforts languished for a long period as other donors held back.

Years later, Robert Decherd stepped up to assume the leadership at the *Dallas Morning News* and its parent, Belo Corporation. Half a century after the assassination, no individual is more responsible than he for today's Sixth Floor Museum at Dealey Plaza.

A descendant of G. B. Dealey, founder of the newspaper and namesake of the plaza, Decherd now is chairman and CEO of today's Belo Corporation media empire. He acknowledged in an interview that the "muscle" of the *News*—financial and otherwise—and the community leadership that its quiet influence brought along—was a critical key to the museum's ultimate realization.

Decherd was a twelve-year-old student in the sixth grade of exclusive St. Mark's boys school when he heard that President Kennedy had been killed and Governor Connally critically wounded. He even remembers what class he was attending (mathematics) and which chair he occupied.

But it wasn't until he accompanied his parents to visit Governor Connally at Parkland Hospital that he realized the magnitude of the tragedy and its personal impact on his family. His father, Benjamin Decherd, was editor of the *News* at the time and was a friend of the governor.

Mindful both of the controversial nature of the museum endeavor and some negative views toward the *News*, Decherd and a few allies played a vital backstage role, providing infrastructure and management expertise while preservation leader Lindalyn Adams, her board and committee members, and other preservation experts remained the out-front public faces.

"Robert's and the *News'* support was absolutely critical to the project's success," Adams said. "It made the difference when the going was tough."

Indeed, when the fund-raising effort still was short of its needs to complete the project, Decherd joined former County Judge Dave Fox to sign a $300,000 bank note to finish the job. The loan was retired through subsequent community donations.

Although he previously never had talked about it, Decherd revealed that, beyond the obvious community need for the museum, he also was motivated by personal distress at watching the proud name of his family soiled by an act forever linked in the public mind to Dealey Plaza.

That grassy fifteen-acre oasis that quickly become infamous around the world is named in honor of his great-grandfather, George Bannerman Dealey.

An early publisher of the *News* and a prominent civic leader, the elder Dealey was instrumental in development of a city plan as early as 1910 that included construction of a levee system to control flooding on the Trinity River. That plan also resulted in the convergence of the three downtown streets that transverse Dealey Plaza. The Art Deco–styled project, built in part by the Depression-era Works Progress Administration, was designated a city park on August 29, 1935, and was named Dealey Plaza.

Reflecting further on the company's key role, Robert Decherd acknowledged that the motivation to support the Sixth Floor Museum project could be in part—consciously or unconsciously—a sort of personal compensation for the

JFK'S FINAL HOURS IN TEXAS

blame that some assigned to the *News* for the notorious ad, unfair as that might be.

The City of Dallas completed major restoration work on Dealey Plaza in early 2013 in preparation for a fiftieth anniversary observance ceremony to be conducted on the site on November 22, 2013.

||||||||||||||||||||||||||||||||||||||||||||||||||||||||||||||||||||||||||||||||||||||||||||||||||||||||||||||||||||||||||||||

CHAPTER TWENTY-ONE

UNLIKELY ALLIES IN TRAGEDY RECOVERY

When I first heard that a sports team and a television soap opera series were credited for being major influences in healing the battered image of Dallas, I was incredulous.

That, however, is the reality that came to pass, Dallas community leaders largely agree.

As already related, the very mention of the city's name following the assassination provoked response ranging from cool silence to outright belligerence. The tragedy had deeply poisoned the public perception of Dallas. Wherever Dallasites traveled, they might well have to endure the scorn and anger of acquaintances and strangers alike.

But by the early 1970s, well after city fathers pushed Mayor Jonsson's Goals for Dallas program as a lofty and meritorious civic endeavor, help came from an unlikely source every year with the arrival of autumn.

A squeaky-clean hero of a quarterback named Roger

Staubach captured the nation's fancy as he led the Dallas Cowboys football team through a golden era that gained it the title of "America's Team."

After a stellar career as quarterback for the United States Naval Academy, during which he was awarded the Heisman Trophy, Staubach was drafted by the Dallas Cowboys in 1964. But it would be years later, due to his military commitment, that he would actually wear a Cowboys uniform. After military service that included time in Vietnam, Staubach began playing professionally with the Cowboys in 1969 under legendary coach Tom Landry.

By the fall of 1971, Staubach was on his way to one of the most remarkable careers in professional football history. After nine consecutive victories that fall, he led the Cowboys to their first Super Bowl win on January 16, 1972, against the Miami Dolphins. It would be the first of two such victories in five Super Bowl appearances while he played under Landry until 1979.

One of the most exciting NFL players of the 1970s, Staubach ignited passion in fans all across the nation. He attracted such nicknames as "Roger the Dodger," because of his scrambling abilities, and "Captain Comeback," for his fourth-quarter heroics. He led the Cowboys to twenty-three fourth-quarter scoring drives that produced late victories, including seventeen of those that came in the last two minutes of the game or in overtime.

The growing fame and affectionate following for the Cowboys became a conversation piece far beyond Texas. Gradually, traveling Dallas residents began to meet increasing numbers of people who wanted to talk with them about Staubach, Landry, and the Cowboys rather than about Dallas as the site of the Kennedy assassination.

A few years later, in 1978, an even more unlikely and

unconventional image-enhancer rode to the city's rescue in the characters of the ribald television soap opera *Dallas*, which aired every Sunday evening on the CBS network.

Set on a fictitious Texas ranch called Southfork, the weekly saga served up rich—and often salacious—helpings of conflict, intrigue, and chicanery built around the wealthy, colorful, and thoroughly fictional Ewing family.

The long-running show attained such popularity, especially outside the United States, that it became the new image of Texas and Dallas in the minds of many. Easterners began to believe that all Texans lived on a ranch or owned an oil well.

A prominent Dallas newsman remembers conducting an interview in London, where his subject asked, in all seriousness, "Do you know the Ewings?"

Community leaders welcomed the new perceptions of their city that had sprung up from unlikely sources, regardless of how they themselves felt about either the Cowboys or the Ewings. The new image, whatever its foundations, was better than what it replaced.

Years later, in 2012, the *Dallas* series was revived on the TNT network, picking up the storyline through another generation of Ewings. A March 2013 episode featured the mysterious death and funeral services of family anti-hero/villain J. R. Ewing. It mirrored the actual death of actor Larry Hagman from cancer in late 2012.

Even today, a tour of the make-believe Southfork ranch outside of Dallas remains a hot ticket for tourists from around the world.

CHAPTER TWENTY-TWO

||||||||||||||||||||||||||||||||||||||||||||||||||||||||||||||||||||||||||||||||||||||||||||||||||||||||||||||

DEALEY PLAZA AND THE SIXTH FLOOR MUSEUM TODAY

As the fiftieth anniversary of the Kennedy assassination passes, Dealey Plaza and the Sixth Floor Museum remain the epicenters of interest in that tragedy.

At virtually any hour of the day or night, the curious still come, often in clusters, but many times alone. They mill around the plaza area in front of the former Texas School Book Depository building and take in the scene they have seen countless times in newspapers and on television. Then, they invariably crane their necks and look skyward for a glimpse of the infamous sixth floor window, usually speaking in hushed tones as they relive the fatal event in their mind's eye. Many produce a cell phone to record the view or ask a bystander to photograph them in front of the building.

Of course, most people have no concept of the proud history of the plaza itself, as related in an earlier chapter, before it became forever linked with a world tragedy.

After absorbing the plaza scene, today's visitors often

find their way to the entrance of the Sixth Floor Museum at the rear of the building. From there they proceed to the sixth floor itself and experience a detailed account of the assassination through an array of photographs and videos, along with contextual material of the era.

When the museum—originally represented as an exhibit—opened in 1989, leaders were duly cautious about content regarding such a sensitive subject, unsure as to how it would be received or interpreted. Many community members doubted the kind of appeal the exhibit would have and felt that the entire mission was unworthy and unwise. They reluctantly accepted the concept, convinced that curiosity would fade away in a few years. Despite such doubts, the exhibit received decisive public approval from diverse crowds of all ages from its opening day forth.

Museum Director Nicola Longford stresses that from the outset, the institution always has been careful to present only material proven to be factual. The exhibit does include a panel describing several major conspiracy theories, but no opinions or conclusions are offered. Officials emphasize that the exhibit was not designed to resolve any controversies surrounding the assassination but rather to help people understand what happened that day.

That neutrality of judgment notwithstanding, Sixth Floor Museum officials readily concede that the public's endless fascination with conspiracies has stimulated enduring interest in the museum.

Curator Gary Mack recounts that museum attendance spiked sharply in 1991 with the release of film director Oliver Stone's controversial movie *JFK*, which presented a conspiracy theory that created a popular sensation.

"He turned an historic event into a current mystery," Mack said, "and I see no signs that the interest will diminish."

The museum board reluctantly had granted Stone access to the sixth floor corner window from which Lee Harvey Oswald fired the assassination shots. For the privilege of less than ten minutes of filming, board leader Dave Fox extracted $50,000 from Stone, funds that were used to retire the remaining debt on the project.

After seeing the completed film, the board declined to permit listing of its name among the credits.

Stone was the last filmmaker to be granted access to the corner window, despite a never-ending stream of requests from media to photograph from the infamous vantage point.

In fact, the museum board subsequently adopted a policy to prohibit entry by any other than museum personnel as a measure to preserve the integrity of the site. Souvenir hunters already had chipped away fragments of surrounding brick walls in the days immediately following the tragedy.

Of course, half a century later, the view from that window still captures the interest of young and old alike. And most people are not aware that the public can have that view today by accessing EarthCam.net on the Internet, thanks to a tiny camera discreetly hidden in one of the boxes stacked near the window.

As a little-known sidelight to plans to install that camera, the late Senator Ted Kennedy, brother of the fallen president, was greatly upset upon hearing an erroneous report that the view presented by the camera was to be as if through the crosshairs of a gunsight. He withdrew his criticism after then-museum director Jeff West rushed to Washington to assure the senator's staff that there were no such plans.

Associate Curator Stephen Fagin has seen an increasing lack of knowledge in today's visitors concerning both the history and the facts about the assassination, especially among younger people.

"We see many young students who do not even recognize the names of those involved," says Fagin. He still recalls the young woman who said that she knew about Kennedy being shot, and *Gerald Ford* becoming president.

"But they all are captivated by the mystery of who killed the president, and once they get here, they become interested in the full story," Fagin said.

Curator Mack, himself a confessed conspiracy theory buff, still believes there is more to the story but never has heard an answer he can accept. He says that more than two-thirds of today's visitors still share a view that supports some kind of conspiracy.

Regardless of conflicting public opinion, the museum is a repository of a remarkable collection of oral histories related to the assassination and its aftermath.

Fagin has overseen more than 1,000 personal video interviews of individuals involved in the period. Participants include such prominent Dallas leaders as former Mayor Erik Jonsson, developer John Stemmons, merchant Stanley Marcus, and former Texas First Lady Nellie Connally.

I recorded my own oral history there with Fagin at his request in 1993 and a supplement to it in 2013. Those resources of fascinating firsthand experiences and viewpoints are available by appointment to researchers and scholars in the reading room of the museum.

Visitors to the Sixth Floor Museum present a wide-ranging spectrum, from the unidentified to the world-famous. One of the most fascinating that Mack remembers was former Soviet Premier Mikhail Gorbachev, who was in Dallas for the State Fair of Texas. He dropped in for a visit with only twenty minutes' notice. Mack was impressed with the premier's knowledge and interest.

Their conversation turned to the inevitable question about a possible conspiracy.

"I was in my first year with the KGB [the notorious Soviet secret police]," Gorbachev said. "I knew our guys didn't do it. We thought maybe your guys did it."

Mack said that Gorbachev then added an ominous afterthought: "And we were ready [for whatever unfolded]."

Museum officials say that some members of the Kennedy family have made discreet, unpublicized visits to the exhibits.

With the fiftieth anniversary milestone of the assassination soon to be a past event, the museum continues to rank as Dallas's most frequented historic attraction, with attendance remaining stable at about 350,000 visitors a year. Their experiences and observations are registered through sometimes-voluminous handwritten entries on the pages of comment books.

‖‖

CHAPTER TWENTY-THREE

NEVER-ENDING CONSPIRACY THEORIES

Fifty years after the Kennedy assassination, the questions persist.

Was it really Lee Harvey Oswald who killed President John F. Kennedy with shots fired from the Texas School Book Depository in downtown Dallas?

If so, was he acting alone? Who may have conspired with him?

Was there, in fact, some larger, sinister plot in which he merely was the trigger man?

The Warren Commission, with members appointed by Kennedy's successor, President Lyndon Johnson, reported in September and November 1964 after a yearlong study that Oswald indeed was the killer and that he acted alone. Years later, in 1978, another congressional panel, the House Select Committee on Assassinations, disputed some of the Warren Commission's conclusions after staging a reenactment of the crime on Dallas streets. It suggested that others must have been involved. Later still, in 1988, the Department of Justice concluded that there were no new trails of evidence to justify further investigation.

Regardless of official findings, conspiracy theories still persist as many continue to believe that there is some missing element to the story. As the fiftieth anniversary milestone approached, Robert Kennedy Jr., nephew of the fallen president, told a Dallas audience in late 2012 that "there is compelling evidence that Oswald did not act alone."

The Sixth Floor Museum avoids taking a position in the controversy, acknowledging the existence of the theories without expressing credence in any of them. A panel in the museum lists a number of individuals and/or entities most mentioned as possibly having been involved in some way. They include the Soviet government/KGB; the Cuban government; a New Orleans scenario that includes the Mafia; anti-Castro elements; the American far right; organized crime in the United States; and Jack Ruby, Oswald's assassin.

Governor Connally always said privately and publicly that he doubted any of the theories because he did not believe that anyone would have been able to keep such an involved secret for this long.

In the course of writing about the fifty-year history of the assassination and its aftermath, I have encountered two of the theories more personally.

The first of these came to me through a call from a student at a North Texas university. For his thesis he was seriously exploring a theory that the driver of the presidential limousine in Dallas had been switched (how, was unclear) and that upon nearing the triple underpass, the new driver turned and shot Kennedy through the head from the front seat.

The theory continued that Governor Connally, seated in front of Kennedy, then pulled a pistol from a leg holster that he habitually wore, fatally shooting the driver. The plot went on: an eyewitness hospital official at Parkland reported that three—not two—bodies were carried to the emergency rooms, and that the supposed deceased assassin ended up in Connally's room but could not be found later.

The author, quite serious and apparently completely sincere, sought my input on the theory.

Although I thought the scenario to be hilarious had it not built on so tragic a subject, I adopted the seriousness of the author and pointed out why I considered it preposterous in every aspect.

First, ignoring the ability of an imposter to take the wheel of the presidential limousine amid a sea of Secret Service agents and Dallas police, I informed him that I had been in close personal contact with Governor Connally on countless occasions over a span of more than thirty years and that I never witnessed nor ever heard of his wearing a pistol holster on his leg. Beyond that fact, I pointed out that Bill Stinson, the governor's travel aide, was with him constantly after the Dallas shooting—even in the operating room—while Nellie Connally and I kept our vigil in the hallway just outside the room. None of us ever saw or heard of a third body.

I must have been somewhat persuasive. The last I heard from the graduate student, he still was pursuing the subject for his thesis, but he had later acknowledged some doubt of his own in the veracity of his dark theory.

I encountered a far more serious theory by accident through a Houston physician who performed surgery on my spine.

"Yes, there was a conspiracy," he told me matter-of-factly.

"But it wasn't about who killed the president. It was about the cover-up on the autopsy afterward."

He then told me of the account of a physician friend who had been on duty at Parkland at the time. My surgeon said that his friend had witnessed Kennedy aides commandeering the president's body from hands of the Dallas County coroner to transport it back to Washington for the autopsy. (Texas law requires an autopsy in the governmental jurisdiction where a violent or questionable death occurs.)

According to the Parkland physician source, the Kennedy aides feared that an independent autopsy would reveal that the president did indeed suffer from Addison's disease, a rumor that had dogged him for years. Ironically, it was his Texas host, Governor John Connally, who years before had been bitterly criticized by Kennedy forces for allegedly circulating rumors of Kennedy's illness in 1960 when he was managing Lyndon Johnson's campaign against Kennedy for the Democratic nomination. Ultimately, of course, Kennedy selected Johnson as his running mate, a decision bitterly opposed by brother Bobby and other Kennedy loyalists, but one that led to his election victory.

With the fiftieth anniversary of the assassination approaching, there undoubtedly will be new theories for conspiracy followers to absorb and deliberate and after that, for as long as the Kennedy assassination is remembered within our society.

||||||||||||||||||||||||||||||||||||||||||||||||||||||||||||||||||||||||||||||||||||||||||||||||||||||

CHAPTER TWENTY-FOUR

THE LARGER LEGACY OF NOVEMBER 22, 1963

As Dallas, Fort Worth, the rest of Texas, and the nation observe the fiftieth anniversary of the John F. Kennedy assassination, what are the legacies of that indelible page of history?

Superficially, the two cities and the state will feel better— as they should—in demonstrating that they have come to grips with the tragedy through a series of historic landmarks and tasteful presentations that both reflect and assuage the pain that they endured for many years following the event. The collective psyche of the communities and nation is softened in the passing of many older citizens who harbored such personal emotions of that day.

Today's generation will never be able to fully appreciate the anguish of that time. Hopefully, this fiftieth milestone will help remaining eyewitnesses to that time to turn the page at last.

Of course, Fort Worth never tasted the full bitter blame

and belligerence visited on Dallas, because it was associated with only the happy hours of the presidential visit there. Any current assessment of either city and of Texas as a state will, of course, find that the region has grown and prospered in every measure since that dark time, despite any stigma sustained fifty years ago.

Dallas in 2013 has become one of the nation's most vibrant cities, harboring a score of Fortune 500 companies, and it enjoys a vital culture of business sophistication. Its Dallas Cowboys, credited with helping change the city's image to the home of "America's Team," now play their games in the nation's most sumptuous sports palace midway between the two cities, in Arlington; and even their unlikely partner in image redemption, the gaudy soap opera *Dallas*, is back on television in a revival series.

Neighboring Fort Worth has enjoyed a dramatic renaissance of its center city while retaining its appealing Old West flavor and friendliness. The prominent and wealthy Bass brothers, descendants of legendary Texas oil pioneer Sid Richardson, have redeveloped blocks of downtown, including the elegant Bass Performance Hall. As a result, the district has evolved into a popular residential address. More recently, local oil billionaire Bob Simpson, who sold his XTO energy company to ExxonMobil, has made history by purchasing and restoring several historic downtown buildings, including the former home of the *Fort Worth Star-Telegram* newspaper.

Among other advancements after the assassination, the two cities finally reconciled their decades-long rivalry to build the vast jointly owned Dallas/Fort Worth International Airport. Larger than the whole of Manhattan Island, it has become a gigantic economic engine that has fueled development of the surrounding metroplex that now numbers more than 6.5 million citizens. It recently was listed as one of the fastest-growing areas in the nation.

Two hundred miles to the south, Austin has become one of the fastest-growing cities and most coveted addresses in the nation for its cutting-edge technology interests and its laid-back lifestyle.

On a broader scale, the state of Texas became an economic bellwether of the early twenty-first century and the nation's bright spot throughout the recent economic downturn. In early 2013, it recorded the largest jobs increase in the United States. Population growth was so robust in the 2000–2010 decade that redistricting following the 2010 Census resulted in Texas gaining four additional seats in Congress.

Many observers believe that some of the credit for the Texas economic growth should go to Governor John Connally for his leadership in achieving sweeping advances in higher education decades earlier to help sow the seeds for prosperity.

Long after the Dallas tragedy and completion of his term as governor, Connally remained an attractive figure on the public scene. President Richard Nixon was so impressed with Connally that he had hoped to name him as his vice president to succeed the resigned Spiro Agnew in 1973. Even after being overrun by his own Watergate problems that prevented such an outcome, Nixon described Connally in his memoirs as the only man in either party who "had the potential to be a great president."

Connally did reach for the brass ring of the White House himself in 1980, but he could not buck the powerful tide of Ronald Reagan.

Retiring from politics, Connally joined political protégé Ben Barnes in an ambitious Texas real estate venture. However, his vision in public policy could not foresee the financial meltdown in the late 1980s that drowned them in debt and led to bankruptcy.

But even in that hour, the handsome silver-haired Texan drew admiration for the courage and dignity that he and Nellie Connally displayed as they watched a lifetime of possessions go under the auctioneer's gavel. Even longtime political foes tipped their hats.

The accession of Lyndon Johnson to the presidency led to the development of the Lyndon B. Johnson Presidential Library and Museum in Austin, in which repose vast archives of the Kennedy assassination. The library recently completed (under the direction of Director Mark Updegrove and LBJ Foundation Chairman Larry Temple) a major update in time for the commemoration of the fiftieth anniversary of the Johnson presidency. It was the first presidential library in Texas when it opened in 1971 (and is now the most visited in the nation), to be followed by the George H. W. Bush Presidential Library and Museum in College Station in 1997 and the George W. Bush Presidential Library and Museum in Dallas, which opened in the spring of 2013. Texas is the only state with three presidential libraries. The John F. Kennedy Presidential Library in Boston, Massachusetts, was not opened until 1979.

Sadly, Lyndon Johnson had precious little time to enjoy his library. He and Lady Bird dedicated the facility on May 22, 1971. But it was only a few months later, on December 12, 1972, that he made his last public appearance as he spoke at the Civil Rights Forum at the library. He slipped a nitroglycerin tablet under his tongue as he addressed the crowd, a clue as to what was to come. Only weeks later, he died at his ranch of a massive heart attack on January 22, 1973.

The larger legacy of November 22 impinges on the entire nation. The death of President Kennedy, the succession of Vice President Lyndon B. Johnson to the presidency, and the subsequent election of Johnson in 1964 enabled the most significant domestic policy developments of the twentieth century. They were highlighted, most notably, by the completion of the passage of civil rights legislation, passage of the Voting Rights Act, and a broad collection of Great Society measures.

But those remarkable milestones depended on both Kennedy and Johnson.

John Kennedy had the vision, conviction, and will to pursue the landmark legislation but seemed to lack the political skill and power to have it enacted. At the time of his death in 1963, only a portion of the civil rights initiative had been passed, and resistance to his further efforts in Congress had stiffened.

Vice President Johnson, on the other hand, was the mastermind of the Senate, legendary for his powers of persuasion; yet, marginalized in the Kennedy administration, he lacked the position of power to carry out anything.

But that changed in Dallas on November 22.

In short order, Johnson moved to complete stalled civil rights legislation and enacted numerous Great Society programs that Kennedy had espoused. Then, following his landslide election victory in 1964, Johnson persuaded, cajoled, and threatened members of Congress to enact the historic Voting Rights Act. The 1964 election gave him sixty-seven votes in the U.S. Senate, a majority never achieved otherwise by either party.

Only those close to Johnson knew how deeply and emotionally he was committed to helping the underprivileged of society. It was a passion that he traced back to his first job, teaching young and poverty-stricken Mexican American children in a South Texas school. He had always known what he wanted to do. Now, with the power, he seized the moment.

However, it took both the death of Kennedy and his

resulting martyrdom to catalyze and enable LBJ's legislative genius to complete the task. Importantly, that milestone legislative accomplishment led to another piece of the legacy from Kennedy's assassination.

If either President Kennedy or Johnson could see today's nation half a century later, they would be pleased, if not surprised, that those legislative actions have led directly to the election of the first African American president in our history.

However, they would perhaps be dismayed to learn the outcome of a prediction by President Johnson. He had warned aides that with passage of civil rights and voting rights legislation, the Democratic Party would lose the South in elections for a generation or more. His prophecy came true in dramatic fashion. The "Solid South" of the past was gone in one election.

In his own state of Texas, all but one statewide official and all but ten members of the 181-member Texas Legislature were Democrats in the 1960s. Seventeen members of Congress flew to Texas with President Kennedy on Air Force One in 1963. All were Democrats.

In 2013, every statewide official in Texas is a Republican, and both the state House and state Senate are controlled by Republicans. The story is virtually the same all across the South.

Johnson and Kennedy would be even more distressed that with this sea change, the very premise of the social contract assumed by the nation for generations is under attack, and the legislative achievements of their era are being eroded. Numerous factions and voices of today espouse going in another direction with vastly different public policies.

In a very real way, Lee Harvey Oswald may have helped change the course of history more than he ever could have imagined.

||||||||||||||||||||||||||||||||||||||||||||||||||||||||||||||||||||||||||||||||||||||||||||||||||||||||||||||||||||||||||||||||||||

WHAT MIGHT HAVE BEEN

A s I look back on my personal memories of November 22, 1963, and the many months of research into the aftermath of that tragedy, I find it hard to believe that fifty years have passed since that indelible time in our history.

Despite all those years, the experiences of those awful hours—from hearing the shots in Dealey Plaza to the long and fitful days and nights in Parkland Hospital—remain as vivid as ever. Reliving them still brings chills. The emotions never go away.

The only gratifying memory that endures is that the life of my close personal friend Governor Connally was spared. Following his recovery, he went on to lead Texas through a period of advancements in education still unrivaled five decades later.

But beyond the enormity and anguish of the tragedy itself, I find myself reflecting on a range of interrelated bittersweet thoughts, even though far secondary to the sadness of John F. Kennedy's death.

They center on what might have been.

I regret that the president did not get to witness the surprise of seeing the huge crowd of Dallasites awaiting him at the Trade Mart, only a few miles from where he died. That turnout decried the "Dallas hate" characterization of the community. Likewise, those gathered there were denied the president's charm that was absorbed by their Fort Worth neighbors just hours earlier.

It was equally regrettable that the president and first lady could not savor the triumph and euphoria of the gala dinner that awaited them in Austin, where so many people already had gathered from across the vast state.

I am sorry that the first couple did not get to spend the night at the LBJ Ranch in Stonewall, and experience the charm of a Lyndon Johnson barbecue on the banks of the Pedernales River the next day. I am sorry that Jackie did not get to wear her new Justin boots there.

On a grander scale, even a half century later, I join countless other citizens in wondering what might have lain ahead in the seductive Camelot narrative.

But try as we might, we cannot change the fateful course of history. However, despite the melancholia that must accompany the fiftieth milestone, I take comfort in the multiple expressions of honor for the fallen president that were planned in Texas as the fiftieth anniversary approached.

They include a respectful ceremony at Dealey Plaza in Dallas, initiated by Mayor Mike Rawlings, exhibitions at the Dallas Museum of Art and the Amon Carter Museum in Fort Worth of the fine art assembled for the Kennedy's Hotel Texas stay in Fort Worth, and a new JFK Tribute plaza in downtown Fort Worth. Other activities also were planned throughout the state.

In a real sense, this chorus of gestures gives fresh expression fifty years later to the last words John F. Kennedy heard from Nellie Connally in the ill-fated motorcade: "Mr. President, you certainly can't say that Dallas [and Texas] doesn't love you."

APPENDIX A

||||||||||||||||||||||||||||||||||||||||||||||||||||||||||||||||||||||||||||||||||||||||||||||||||||||||||||||||||||||||||||

WHITE HOUSE PRESS SCHEDULE

FOR YOUR INFORMATION AND IMMEDIATE USE

November 20, 1963

Office of the White House Press Secretary

- -

THE WHITE HOUSE

SCHEDULE OF THE PRESIDENT
TEXAS, NOV. 21–22, 1963

WEDNESDAY, NOVEMBER 20, 1963

9:00 p.m. deadline on baggage. Baggage can be
left at the White House Transportation Office
any time in the afternoon.

THURSDAY, NOVEMBER 21, 1963

8:30 a.m.   Press check in at the White House

9:00 a.m.   Press buses leave Northwest Gate of the White House

10:00 a.m.   Press plane departs Andrews AFB

10:45 a.m.   PRESIDENT DEPARTS WHITE HOUSE BY
               HELICOPTER FOR ANDREWS AFB
               Pool: Smith, Cormier, Costello, Mathias

11:00 a.m.   PRESIDENT DEPARTS ANDREWS AFB

12:30 p.m.   Press plane arrives San Antonio International Airport

1:30 p.m.	PRESIDENT ARRIVES SAN ANTONIO INTERNATIONAL AIRPORT
1:40 p.m.	PRESIDENT DEPARTS SAN ANTONIO INTERNATIONAL AIRPORT BY CAR
2:25 p.m.	PRESIDENT ARRIVES AERO-SPACE MEDICAL HEALTH CENTER, BROOKS AFB
2:30 p.m.	Dedication program begins
3:05 p.m.	PRESIDENT DEPARTS AERO-SPACE MEDICAL HEALTH CENTER BY CAR FOR KELLY AFB
3:00 p.m. [sic]	PRESIDENT ARRIVES KELLY AFB
3:30 p.m.	PRESIDENT DEPARTS KELLY AFB Pool: Merriman Smith, UPI; Frank Cormier, AP; Felton West, Houston Post; Robert MacNeil, NBC
4:15 p.m.	PRESIDENT ARRIVES HOUSTON INTERNATIONAL AIRPORT
4:25 p.m.	PRESIDENT DEPARTS AIRPORT BY CAR
5:00 p.m.	PRESIDENT ARRIVES RICE HOTEL
8:35 p.m.	DEPART RICE HOTEL BY CAR Pool: Merriman Smith, UPI; Frank Cormier, AP; William MacKay, Houston Chronicle; Sid Davis, Westinghouse.
8:45 p.m.	PRESIDENT ARRIVES COLISEUM TO ATTEND CONGRESSMAN ALBERT THOMAS DINNER
9:30 p.m.	PRESIDENT DEPARTS COLISEUM BY CAR
9:55 p.m.	PRESIDENT ARRIVES HOUSTON INTERNATIONAL AIRPORT
10:00 p.m.	PRESIDENT DEPARTS AIRPORT
10:45 p.m.	PRESIDENT ARRIVES CARSWELL AFB, FORT WORTH
10:50 p.m.	PRESIDENT DEPARTS CARSWELL AFB BY CAR
11:10 p.m.	PRESIDENT ARRIVES TEXAS HOTEL, FORT WORTH

FRIDAY, NOVEMBER 22, 1963

8:45 a.m.   PRESIDENT ATTENDS BREAKFAST IN TEXAS
              HOTEL SPONSORED BY THE FORT WORTH
              CHAMBER OF COMMERCE
              Pool: Merriman Smith, UPI; Frank Cormier, AP;
              Bob Baskin, Dallas News; Bob Clark, ABC

9:45 a.m.   PRESIDENT RETURNS TO ROOM

10:30 a.m.   PRESIDENT DEPARTS TEXAS HOTEL
              BY MOTOR

11:05 a.m.   PRESIDENT ARRIVES CARSWELL AFB

11:15 a.m.   PRESIDENT DEPARTS CARSWELL AFB BY JET

11:35 a.m.   PRESIDENT ARRIVES LOVE FIELD, DALLAS

11:45 a.m.   PRESIDENT DEPARTS LOVE FIELD BY MOTOR

12:30 p.m.   PRESIDENT ARRIVES TRADE MART TO
              ATTEND LUNCHEON SPONSORED BY THE
              DALLAS CITIZENS COUNCIL, THE DALLAS
              ASSEMBLY AND THE GRADUATE RESEARCH
              CENTER OF THE SOUTHWEST

2:00 p.m.   PRESIDENT DEPARTS TRADE MART BY MOTOR
              Pool: Merriman Smith, UPI; Frank Cormier, AP;
              Bob Pierpoint, CBS; Chuck Roberts, Newsweek

2:30 p.m.   PRESIDENT ARRIVES LOVE FIELD

2:35 p.m.   PRESIDENT DEPARTS LOVE FIELD BY JET

3:15 p.m.   PRESIDENT ARRIVES BERGSTROM AFB, Austin

3:30 p.m.   PRESIDENT DEPARTS BERGSTROM AFB BY
              MOTOR

3:55 p.m.   PRESIDENT ARRVIES COMMODORE PERRY
              HOTEL, AUSTIN

4:15 p.m.   PRESIDENT ATTENDS RECEPTION IN
              COMMODORE PERRY HOTEL SPONSORED
              BY THE DEMOCRATIC STATE COMMITTEE
              (no press coverage)

6:00 p.m.   PRESIDENT DEPARTS COMMODORE PERRY
              HOTEL BY MOTOR

6:05 p.m.	PRESIDENT ARRIVES GOVERNOR'S MANSION TO ATTEND RECEPTION (no press coverage)
6:45 p.m.	PRESIDENT DEPARTS GOVERNOR'S MANSION BY MOTOR
6:50 p.m.	PRESIDENT ARRIVES COMMODORE PERRY HOTEL
7:30 p.m.	Press buses depart hotel
8:15 p.m.	PRESIDENT DEPARTS COMMODORE PERRY HOTEL BY MOTOR Pool: Merriman Smith, UPI; Frank Cormier, AP; Bob Hollingsworth, Dallas Times–Herald; Bob MacNeil, NBC
8:20 p.m.	PRESIDENT ARRIVES MUNICIPAL AUDITORIUM FOR FUND-RAISING DINNER SPONORED BY THE DEMOCRATIC STATE COMMITTEE (buffet set up for press)
8:30 p.m.	PRESIDENT SEATED AT HEAD TABLE
8:45 p.m.	PROGRAM STARTS
9:15 p.m.	PROGRAM ENDED
9:30 p.m.	PRESIDENT DEPARTS MUNICIPAL AUDITORIUM BY MOTOR
9:45 p.m.	PRESIDENT ARRIVES BERGSTROM AFB
9:50 p.m.	PRESIDENT DEPARTS BERGSTROM AFB BY HELICOPTER
10:20 p.m.	PRESIDENT ARRIVES VICE PRESIDENT JOHNSON'S RANCH

– – – –

PRESS NOTES:

There will be adequate Western Union and telephone facilities at every stop.

The Press Room at the Rice Hotel in Houston is the Colorado & Brazos Rooms with bar and buffet provided as well as a lounge room to freshen up in. The Press Room in the Texas Hotel in Fort Worth is on the mezzanine. In addition there is a working press table at the breakfast as well as a press buffet nearby. In Dallas at the Trade Mart there will be a press room set up on the 4th floor as well as a press luncheon. At Austin the press room is in the basement one flight down from the lobby. Press Room at the auditorium and a press buffet. At the auditorium there are reserved press seats in the balcony.

The press is pre-registered at every hotel stop with a table set up where keys can be obtained.

# # # # #

TRIP OF THE PRESIDENT
to
SAN ANTONIO, HOUSTON, FORT WORTH & DALLAS, TEXAS

November 21–23, 1963

Lv. Washington, D.C. (Andrews AFB).....................11:00 AM EST
Ar. San Antonio, Texas (San Antonio International).........1:30 PM CST

Members of the party,

THE PRESIDENT

Mrs. Jacqueline Kennedy
The Vice-President
Mr. Kenneth O'Donnell
Mr. David Powers
Mr. Lawrence O'Brien
Gen. Chester Clifton
Mr. Malcolm Kilduff
Mr. George Burkley
Mrs. Evelyn Lincoln
Miss Pamela Turnure
Miss Christine Camp
Mrs. Mary Gallagher

Sen. Ralph Yarborough
Cong. Jack Brooks
Cong. Ray Roberts
Cong. Olin Teague
Cong. Albert Thomas
Cong. Homer Thornberry
Cong. Jim Wright
Cong. Graham Purcell
Cong. John Young

Cong. Joe Kilgore
Cong. Walter Rogers
Cong. George Mahon
Cong. Henry Gonzalez
Cong. O. C. Fisher
Cong. Lindley Beckworth
Cong. Wright Patman
Cong. Clark Thompson

PRESS SECTION: PAN AMERICAN WORLD AIRWAYS CHARTER

Lv. Washington, D.C. (Andrews AFB)................... 10:00 AM EST
Ar. San Antonio, Tex. (San Antonio International)..........12:30 PM CST

Atkins, Thomas	Navy–Photos	
Baskin, Robert	Dallas News	
Bell, Jack	Associated Press	
Broder, David	Washington Star	
Brandon, Henry	London Sunday Times	
Burroughs, Henry	Associated Press–Photos	
Cahn, Robert	United States Information Agency	
Cancellare, Frank	United Press International–Photos	
Clark, Robert	American Broadcasting Company	
Cormier, Frank	Associated Press	Pool
Costello, William	Mutual Broadcasting System	
Craven, Thomas Jr.	CBS–TV	
Cromley, Allan	Daily Oklahoman	
Davis, Sid	Westinghouse Broadcasting Company	
Donovan, Robert	Los Angeles Times	
Doyle, Jack	American Telephone & Telegraph Company	
Dudman, Richard	St. Louis Post–Dispatch	
Flaherty, Thomas	Life	
Folliard, Edward T.	Washington Post	
Gertz, Jack	American Telephone & Telegraph Company	
Grant, Clint	Dallas News–Photos	
Healy, Paul	New York Daily News	
Hercher, Wilmot	U. S. News and World Report	
Hilburn, Robert	Ft. Worth Star Telegram	
Hofen, John	NBC–TV	
Hollingsworth, Robert	Dallas Times–Herald	
Kantor, Seth	Scripps–Howard	
Kent, Carleton	Chicago Sun–Times	

Kiker, Douglas	New York Herald Tribune
Lawrence, Fred	UPI–News Film
Linkins, Carroll	Western Union
Lisagor, Peter	Chicago Daily News
MacKaye, William	Houston Chronicle
MacNeil, Robert	National Broadcasting Company
Mathis, James	Newhouse Newspapers
May, William	Newark News
Means, Marianne	Hearst Newspapers
Otten, Alan	Wall Street Journal
Perry, James	National Observer
Pierpoint, Robert	Columbia Broadcasting System
Potter, Philip	Baltimore Sun
Rickerby, Arthur	Life–Photos
Riggs, Robert	Louisville Courier–Journal
Roberts, Charles	Newsweek
Roth, Robert	Philadelphia Bulletin
Ryan, Cleveland	Lighting Technician
Schultz, Jack	UPI–News Film
Sidey, Hugh	Time
Silverman, Alvin	Cleveland Plain Dealer
Smith, Merriman	United Press International Pool
Stoughton, Cecil	WHCA–Photos
TerHorst, Jerry	Detroit News
West, Felton	Houston Post
Wicker, Thomas	New York Times
Wiegman, David	NBC–TV
Williams, Jack	Kansas City Star
Willoner, Andrew	CBS–TV
Young, Robert	Chicago Tribune

JOINERS:

Brogan, Mary Rice	Houston Chronicle
Byers, Bo	Houston Chronicle
Dugger, Ronnie	Texas Observer
Kinch, Sam	Ft. Worth Star–Telegram
Kraft, Gene	KFJZ–Ft. Worth
Neal, Bruce	Wendall Mays Radio Stations
Rozumalski, Ted	Houston Chronicle–Photos
Shelton, Keith	Dallas Times Herald
Tackett, Johnny	Scripps–Howard
Uhlmann, Arthur	Houston Chronicle–Photos

PAN AMERICAN

Captain	Douglas Moody	Purser	Kari-Mette Steiner
First Officer	Ralph Hunt	Purser	Carol Tangen
Second Officer	Carl Gray	Stewardess	Linda Pinkerton
Flight Engineer	Charles Corey	Stewardess	Sheila Riley
Flight Engineer	Robert Piper	Stewardess	Elfriede Zimmerman
Operations Rep.	Nicholas Walters	Stewardess	Catherine Johnson
Commissary Rep.	Charles Mettler	Stewardess	Layte Bowden

‖‖‖

TEXAS WELCOME DINNER SPEECH SCHEDULED FOR DELIVERY BY JOHN F. KENNEDY ON NOVEMBER 22, 1963

One hundred and eighteen years ago last March, President John Tyler signed the Joint Resolution of Congress providing statehood for Texas. And 118 years ago next month, President James Polk declared that Texas was a part of the Union.

Both Tyler and Polk were Democratic Presidents. And from that day to this, Texas and the Democratic Party have been linked in an indestructible alliance—an alliance for the promotion of prosperity, growth, and greatness for Texas and for America.

In 1964 that alliance will sweep this state and nation.

The historic bonds that link Texas and the Democratic Party are no temporary union of convenience. They are deeply embedded in the history and purpose of this state and party. The Democratic Party is not a collection of diverse interests brought together only to win elections. We are united instead by a common history and heritage—by a respect for the deeds of the past and a recognition of the needs of the future.

Never satisfied with today, we have always staked our fortunes on tomorrow. That is the kind of state that Texas has always been— that is the kind of vision and vitality which Texans have always possessed—and that is the reason why Texas will always be basically Democratic.

For 118 years, Texas and the Democratic Party have contributed to each other's success. This state's rise to prosperity and wealth came primarily from the policies and programs of Woodrow Wilson, Franklin Roosevelt, and Harry Truman. Those policies were shaped and enacted with the help of such men as the late Sam Rayburn and a host of other key Congressmen—by the former Texas Congressman and Senator who serves now as my strong right arm, Vice President Lyndon B. Johnson—by your present U.S. Senator, Ralph Yarborough—and by an overwhelming proportion of Democratic leadership at the state and county level, led by your distinguished Governor, John Connally.

It was the policy and programs of the Democratic Party which helped bring income to your farmers, industries to your workers, and the promotion and preservation of your natural resources.

No one who remembers the days of five-cent cotton and thirty-cent oil will forget the ties between the success of this state and the success of our party.

Three years ago this fall I toured this state with Lyndon Johnson, Sam Rayburn, and Ralph Yarborough as your party's candidate for President. We pledged to increase America's strength against its enemies, its prestige among its friends, and the opportunities it offered to its citizens. Those pledges have been fulfilled. The words spoken in Texas have been transformed into action in Washington, and we have America moving again.

Here in Austin, I pledged in 1960 to restore world confidence in the vitality and energy of American society. That pledge has been fulfilled. We have won the respect of allies and adversaries alike through our determined stand on behalf of freedom around the world from West Berlin to Southeast Asia—through our resistance to Communist intervention in the Congo and Communist missiles in Cuba—and through our initiative in obtaining the nuclear test ban treaty which can stop the pollution of our atmosphere and start us on the path to peace again.

In San José and Mexico City, in Bonn and West Berlin, in Rome and County Cork, I saw and heard and felt a new appreciation for an America on the move and an America which has shown it cares about the needy of its own and other lands, an America which has shown that freedom is the way to the future, an America which is known to be first in the effort for peace as well as preparedness.

In Amarillo I pledged in 1960 that the businessmen of this state and nation—particularly the small businessman who is the backbone of our economy—would move ahead as our economy moved ahead. That pledge has been fulfilled. Business profits—having risen 43 percent in two and one-half years—now stand at a record high; and businessmen all over America are grateful for liberalized depreciation, for the investment tax credit, and for our program to increase their markets at home as well as abroad.

We have proposed a massive tax reduction, with particular benefits for small business. We have stepped up the activities of the Small Business Administration, making available in the last three years almost $50 million to more than 1,000 Texas firms, doubling their opportunity to share in federal procurement contracts. Our party believes that what is good for the American people is good for American business—and the last three years have proven the validity of that proposition.

In Grand Prairie, I pledged in 1960 that this country would no longer tolerate the lowest rate of economic growth of any major industrialized nation in the world. That pledge has been and is being fulfilled. In less than three years our national output will shortly have risen by a record $100 billion—industrial production is up 22 percent—personal income is up 16 percent. And the *Wall Street Journal* pointed out a short time ago that the United States now leads most of Western Europe in the rate of business expansion and the margin of corporate profits. Here in Texas—where three years ago, at the very time I was speaking, real per capita personal income was actually declining as the industrial recession spread to this state—more than 200,000 new jobs have been created—unemployment has declined and personal income rose last year to an all-time high. This growth must go on. Those not sharing in this prosperity must be helped. That is why we have an accelerated public works program, an area redevelopment program, and a manpower training program—to keep this and other states moving ahead. And that is why we need a tax cut of $11 billion, as an assurance of future growth and insurance against an early recession. No period of economic recovery in the peacetime history of this nation has been characterized by both the length and strength of our present expansion—and we intend to keep it going.

In Dallas, I pledged in 1960 to step up the development of both our natural and our human resources. That pledge has been fulfilled. The policy of "no new starts" has been reversed. The Canadian

River project will provide water for eleven Texas cities. The San Angelo project will irrigate some 10,000 acres. We have launched ten new watershed projects in Texas, completed seven others, and laid plans for six more. A new national park, a new wildlife preserve, and other navigation, reclamation, and natural resource projects are all under way in this state. At the same time, we have sought to develop the human resources of Texas and all the nation—granting loans to 17,500 Texas college students—making more than $17 million available to 249 school districts—and expanding or providing rural library service to 600,000 Texas readers. And if this Congress passes, as now seems likely, pending bills to build college classrooms, increase student loans, build medical schools, provide more community libraries, and assist in the creation of graduate centers, then this Congress will have done more for the cause of education than has been done by any Congress in modern history. Civilization, it was once said, is a race between education and catastrophe—and we intend to win that race by education.

In Wichita Falls, I pledged in 1960 to increase farm income and reduce the burden of farm surpluses. That pledge has been fulfilled. Net farm income today is almost a billion dollars higher than in 1960. In Texas, net income per farm consistently averaged below the $4,000 mark under the Benson regime—it is now well above it. And we have raised this income while reducing grain surpluses by 1 billion bushels. We have, at the same time, tackled the problem of the entire rural economy—extending more than twice as much credit to Texas farmers under the Farmers Home Administration, and making more than $100 million in REA loans. We have not solved all the problems of American agriculture—but we have offered hope and a helping hand in place of Mr. Benson's indifference.

In San Antonio, I pledged in 1960 that a new administration would strive to secure for every American his full constitutional rights. That pledge has been and is being fulfilled. We have not yet secured the objectives desired or the legislation required. But we have, in the last three years, by working through voluntary leadership as well as legal action, opened more new doors to members of minority groups—doors to transportation, voting, education, employment, and places of public accommodation—than had been opened in any three-year or thirty-year period in this century. There is no noncontroversial way to fulfill our constitutional pledge to establish justice and promote domestic tranquility—but we intend to fulfill those obligations because they are right. In Houston, I pledged in 1960 that we would set before the American people the unfinished business of our society. That pledge has been fulfilled. We have undertaken the first full-scale revision of our tax laws in ten years. We have launched a bold new attack on mental illness, emphasizing treatment in the patient's own home community instead of some vast custodial institution. We have initiated a full-scale attack on mental retardation, emphasizing prevention instead of abandonment. We have revised our public welfare programs, emphasizing family rehabilitation instead of humiliation, and we have proposed a comprehensive realignment of our national transportation policy, emphasizing equal competition instead of regulation. Our agenda is still long—but this country is moving again.

In El Paso, I pledged in 1960 that we would give the highest and earliest priority to the reestablishment of good relations with the people of Latin America. We are working to fulfill that pledge. An area long neglected has not solved all its problems. The Communist foothold which had already been established has not yet been eliminated. But the trend of Communist expansion has been reversed. The name of Fidel Castro is no longer feared or cheered by substantial numbers in every country—and contrary to the prevailing predictions of three years ago, not another inch of Latin American territory has fallen prey to Communist control. Meanwhile, the work of reform and reconciliation goes on. I can testify from my trips to Mexico, Colombia, Venezuela, and Costa Rica that American officials are no longer booed and spat upon south of the border. Historic fences and friendships are being maintained. And Latin America, once the forgotten stepchild of our aid programs, now receives more economic assistance per capita than any other area of the world. In short, the United States is once more identified with the needs and aspirations of the people to the south—and we intend to meet those needs and aspirations.

In Texarkana, I pledged in 1960 that our country would no longer engage in a lagging space effort. That pledge has been fulfilled. We are not yet first in every field of space endeavor—but we have regained worldwide respect for our scientists, our industry, our education, and our free initiative.

In the last three years, we have increased our annual space effort to a greater level than the combined total of all space activities undertaken in the 1950s. We have launched into earth orbit more than four times as many space vehicles as had been launched in the previous three years. We have focused our wide-ranging efforts around a landing on the moon in this decade. We have put valuable weather and communications satellites into actual operation. We will fire this December the most powerful rocket ever developed anywhere in the world. And we have made it clear to all that the United States of America has no intention of finishing second in outer space. Texas will play a major role in this effort. The Manned Space Center in Houston will be the cornerstone of our lunar landing project, with $1 billion already allocated to that center this year. Even though space is an infant industry, more than three thousand people are already employed in space activities here in Texas—more than $100 million of space contracts are now being worked on in this state—and more than fifty space-related firms have announced the opening of Texas offices. This is still a daring and dangerous frontier, and there are those who would prefer to turn back or to take a more timid stance. But Texans have stood their ground on embattled frontiers before—and I know you will help us see this battle through.

In Fort Worth, I pledged in 1960 to build a national defense which was second to none, a position I said, which is not "first, when," but—first period. That pledge has been fulfilled. In the past few years we have increased our defense budget by over 20 percent; increased the program for acquisition of Polaris submarines from twenty-four to forty-one; increased our Minuteman missile purchase program by more than 75 percent; doubled the number of strategic bombers and missiles on alert; doubled the number of nuclear weapons available in the strategic alert forces; increased the tactical nuclear forces deployed in Western Europe by 60 percent; added five combat ready divisions and five tactical fighter wings to our Armed Forces; increased our strategic airlift capabilities by 75 percent; and increased our special counter-insurgency forces by 600 percent. We can truly say today, with pride in our voices and peace in our hearts, that the defensive forces of the United States are, without a doubt, the most powerful and resourceful forces anywhere in the world.

Finally, I said in Lubbock in 1960, as I said in every other speech in this state, that if Lyndon Johnson and I were elected, we would get this country moving again. That pledge has been fulfilled. In nearly every field of national activity, this country is moving again—and Texas is moving with it. From public works to public health, wherever government programs operate, the past three years have seen a new burst of action and progress—in Texas and all over America. We have stepped up the fight against crime and slums and poverty in our cities, against the pollution of our streams, against unemployment in our industry and against waste in the federal government. We have built hospitals, clinics, and nursing homes. We have launched a broad new attack on mental illness and mental retardation. We have initiated the training of more physicians and dentists. We have provided four times as much housing for our elderly citizens—and we have increased benefits for those on social security.

Almost everywhere we look, the story is the same. In Latin America, in Africa, in Asia—in the councils of the world and in the jungles of far-off nations—there is now renewed confidence in our country and our convictions.

For this country is moving, and it must not stop. It cannot stop. This is a time for courage and a time of challenge. Neither conformity nor complacency will do. Neither the fanatics nor the faint-hearted are needed. And our duty as a party is not to our party alone, but to the nation, and indeed to all mankind. Our duty is not merely the preservation of political power but the preservation of peace and freedom.

So let us not be petty when our cause is so great. Let us not quarrel amongst ourselves when our nation's future is at stake. Let us stand together with renewed confidence in our cause—united in our heritage of the past and our hopes for the future—and determined that this land we love shall lead all mankind into new frontiers of peace and abundance.

[*Source: Author's collection, copy of speech printed by the State Democratic Executive Committee of Texas*]

PHOTO CREDITS

58: Courtesy of Gene Gordon.

59: Courtesy of Gene Gordon.

60-61: *Fort Worth Star-Telegram* Collection, courtesy of The University of Texas at Arlington Library Special Collections.

62: Tom Dillard Collection, *Dallas Morning News*, The Sixth Floor Museum at Dealey Plaza.

63: Courtesy *Dallas Morning News* archives.

64-65: Tom Dillard Collection, *Dallas Morning News*, The Sixth Floor Museum at Dealey Plaza.

66-67: Tom Dillard Collection, *Dallas Morning News*, The Sixth Floor Museum at Dealey Plaza.

68-69: William Beal, photographer, *Dallas Times Herald* Collection, The Sixth Floor Museum at Dealey Plaza.

70-71: Jay Skaggs Collection, the Sixth Floor Museum at Dealey Plaza.

72-73: *Dallas Times Herald* Collection, The Sixth Floor Museum at Dealey Plaza.

74: *Fort Worth Star-Telegram* Collection, courtesy of The University of Texas at Arlington Library Special Collections.

75: *Fort Worth Star-Telegram* Collection, courtesy of The University of Texas at Arlington Library Special Collections.

76: Photo by Flip Schulke, Flip Schulke Photographic Archive, di_08158, Dolph Briscoe Center for American History, The University of Texas at Austin.

109: *Fort Worth Star-Telegram* Collection, courtesy of The University of Texas at Arlington Library Special Collections.

110-111: Courtesy *Dallas Morning News* archives.

112-113: Courtesy *Dallas Morning News* archives.

114-115: Courtesy of the LBJ Presidential Library.

116-117: PICA 07066, Austin History Center, Austin Public Library.

118, top: YouTube, http://www.youtube.com/watch?v=fJdCgZAVDEI.

118, bottom: YouTube, http://www.youtube.com/watch?v=kj6jJIwxhxc.

119, top: Author's collection.

119, bottom: Author's collection.

120-121: Author's collection.

122-123: AP Images.

124: AP Images.

125: Author's collection.

126: Courtesy *Dallas Morning News* archives.

127: Courtesy *Dallas Morning News* archives.

128: Courtesy *Dallas Morning News* archives.

129: Courtesy of The Sixth Floor Museum at Dealey Plaza.

130, top: Institutional Archives, The Sixth Floor Museum at Dealey Plaza.

130, bottom: Institutional Archives, The Sixth Floor Museum at Dealey Plaza.

131, top: Institutional Archives, The Sixth Floor Museum at Dealey Plaza.

131, bottom: Institutional Archives, The Sixth Floor Museum at Dealey Plaza.

132: DeGolyer Library, Southern Methodist University, Dallas, Texas, Belo Records, A2010.0001.

133: Courtesy of The Sixth Floor Museum at Dealey Plaza.

134: Courtesy of The Sixth Floor Museum at Dealey Plaza.

135: Courtesy of The Sixth Floor Museum at Dealey Plaza.

136-137: Courtesy of The Sixth Floor Museum at Dealey Plaza.

138: Courtesy of the LBJ Presidential Library.

139: Courtesy of the LBJ Presidential Library.

140: Courtesy Downtown Fort Worth, Inc.

||||||||||||||||||||||||||||||||||||||||||||||||||||||||||||||||||||||||||||||||||||||||||||||||||||||||||

ACKNOWLEDGMENTS

The completion of this book represents the end of a long overdue, fifty-year journey. And, like most journeys, it could not have been traveled but for the help of many associates and friends—and rank strangers—along the way.

The shock and anguish of all that I witnessed during and surrounding the Kennedy assassination remained indelibly seared into my memory for decades. Each November after the tragedy, I coordinated endless media interviews with Governor John Connally to re-live the event until his death in 1983. After that, I fielded and responded to similar requests of Nellie Connally.

But I never have written my own experiences—until now.

One of the first to thank in this endeavor is my late executive assistant, Marla Westfall of Fort Worth. Marla had the presence of mind to collect and file away a heap of documents, news clippings, and crudely scrawled notes from the top of my makeshift desk at Parkland Hospital. She thus preserved my own personal time capsule, unknown to me until it arrived at my Austin office in 1998. The book includes some of that original material, such as a copy of the White House itinerary for the Texas trip and the manifests listing all aboard Air Force One and the chartered White House Press plane. Marla's diligence provided a valuable archive to help start the journey.

Not far behind ranks another Marla—Marla Matthews, a talented Austin public affairs pro and a valued associate at my communications firm, who nagged me without mercy for years to write a book. Marla started the journey with me months ago, formatting and editing initial drafts of manuscripts, and has loyally remained on board through publication (while also busy serving her clients). She was joined by longtime associate Gary Pickle, whose editing added discipline and depth to the text. Loyal friend Ben Flusche offered his always-solid and honest critique, and I also had support from years-long associate Terry Young.

In reconstructing details of the Kennedy trip, I had the benefit of extended interviews with a number of longtime friends, including Neal Spelce, Howard Rose, Will Davis, Larry Temple, Ben Barnes, Jim Wright, Kenneth Barr, Nancy Abington, Cornelia (Corky) Friedman, and Gene Gordon. Several of Gordon's remarkable photographs are included in the book. A behind-the-scenes glimpse of preparations for a visit to the LBJ Ranch came from interviews with Lady Bird Johnson's personal secretary Bess Abell and longtime butler James Davis. The three Connally children—John Connally III, Mark Connally, and Sharon Ammann—were generous in remembering their awful ordeal of their father's struggle for his life.

Beyond the assassination itself, clear and compelling perspectives on the bitter aftermath for Dallas and Texas came via interviews, including those with respected journalists and historians Pierce Allman, Hugh Aynesworth, Darwin Payne, and Wes Wise.

The story of the long journey for Dallas and Texas to recognize and finally come to peace with the tragedy was enriched by the perspectives of key participants and enablers. I am especially indebted to gracious Lindalyn Adams, the unquestioned queen of community historical preservation in Dallas and a longtime personal friend. In addition to lengthy interviews where she shared her rich knowledge of that history and her crucial role in shaping it, she opened doors to the experiences and viewpoints of others who played key parts, including Conover Hunt, Lee Jackson, and Robert Decherd, as well as oral histories of Ted Dealey, Judson Shook, and Erik Jonsson.

I am very grateful for the generous support accorded by the Sixth Floor Museum at Dealey Plaza through the grace of Director Nicola Langford, Curator Gary Mack, and Associate Curator Stephen Fagin. And I appreciate the equal generosity of the LBJ Presidential Library and Museum in Austin though Director Mark Updegrove,

Deputy Director Tina Houston, and longtime personal friend Larry Temple, chairman of the LBJ Foundation.

Special insights to fiftieth anniversary plans and motivations for memorials to President Kennedy have come from Mike Rawlings, Olivier Meslay, Dr. Andrew Walker, Andrew Taft, Dave Fuller, Bill Thornton, Joy Webster, and Shirlee and Taylor Gandy.

I am particularly grateful for the professional skills, courtesy, and patience of a loyal band of photographic researchers who have searched for, found, and provided the outstanding graphic images appearing in the book: Cathy Spitzenberger, University of Texas at Arlington Library; Tom Shelton, University of Texas at San Antonio; Mark Davies and Krishna Shenoy, The Sixth Floor Museum at Dealey Plaza; Matthew Lutts, Associated Press Images, New York; Jerome Sims, *Dallas Morning News*; Joyce Lee, *Houston Chronicle*; Nicole Davis, Austin History Center; Sammie Lee and Adrianne Pierce, Dallas Public Library; Ada Negraru and Pamalla Anderson, DeGolyer Library, Southern Methodist University; Christopher Banks and Margaret Harmon, LBJ Presidential Library and Museum; Zack Ryland and Jay Godwin, *Austin American-Statesman*; Sarah Boynton, Parkland Hospital; and Harry Cabluck, freelance photographer, retired, Associated Press.

I could not complete any list of indebtedness without thanking the trusty Samaritans who rescued me from my personal technology impairment and periodic computer hiccups along the journey. They include Cohn & Wolfe associates Temple Barron, Karen Marino, and Chris Hightower, along with my daughters, Courtney Read Hoffman and Ellen Read. And I appreciate the advice of my consummate book reader friend and Kennedy historian Fraser Croft.

I always will be grateful to Evan Smith for his valuable counsel and assistance, and I extend the same sentiment to Steve Bercu. I also have special gratitude for Dave Hamrick at the University of Texas Press in Austin for his critical advice and generous help, and for the excellent work on this project of the talented Regina Fuentes and Derek George.

Finally, I am very proud to partner with the respected Dolph Briscoe Center for American History as publisher of the book. I have high regard for Executive Director Don Carleton, its passionate advocate for history, and am deeply grateful to him and his able publishing team of Erin Purdy and Holly Taylor for guiding my contribution to reality. Equal thanks go to Arthur Klebanoff at Rosetta Books in New York as publisher of the electronic edition, and to Sandi Mendelson for her marketing support.

I also offer thanks to many other friends for their interest and support, along with apologies to any who may inadvertently have been overlooked.

Julian Read

August 12, 2013

INDEX

Mart, 36; interest in Sixth
Floor Museum, 155; management of, 38–39; plans for Texas
visit, 13–14; reporting immediately after shooting, 36
press bus, 7–8, 35–36, *70–71*
press room, temporary, 40,
72–73, 74
press schedule, 189–196
priest, Catholic, 40
protocol, 94–95
Pryor, Cactus, 29, 83
public, grief of, 1–2, 81, 82–83
public relations business, 2

R
rain, 26–27
rally, partisan: JFK at, *58, 59*;
planning for, 14–15, 19; success
of, 8, 31–32
Rawlings, Mike, 186
Read, Anice, 44
Read, Courtney, 44
Read, Ellen, 44, 103
Read, Julian: campaign advisor,
3–5; in coffee shop, 24; at Dallas Trade Mart, 37; decision to
go to Dallas, 33–34; on Jacqueline Kennedy, 33; managing
press, 36, 42, 97–98, 143–144;
with Nellie Connally, *125*; Nellie Connally's book tour, 103;
oral history contribution, 173;
at Parkland Hospital, 37–40,
40–41, *74, 120–121*; pride of,
2; public relations/advertis-
ing business, 2; reflections
on assassination, 185–187;
relationship with Connally,

4–5, 31; seeing Oswald, 94;
witnessing assassination, 2,
35–36, 44
Reagan, Ronald, 154, 180
Republican Party, 20, 107–108,
184
research facility dedication,
22–23, *50, 51*
Reynolds, Dick, 90–91
Richardson, Sid, 180
Robinson, Hugh, 155
Rose, Howard, 82, 90, 100
Ruby, Jack, 79, 93–94, 176

S
Salant, Richard "Dick," 98, *119*
San Antonio, Texas, 14, 22–23,
48–49
schism, 11–12, 20
Schulke, Flip, *76*
Secret Service, 9, 17, 18, 24, 28,
81, 85, 86, 94, 177
security: concern about Dallas
visit, 25–26; motorcade
concerns, 19–20; at Parkland
Hospital, 37, 92
Sellers, Richard, 156, 157
Shaw, Robert, 41, 42, 99
Shook, C. Judson, Jr.: enlisting
Adams for Sixth Floor
Museum, 151; preservation of
Texas School Book Depository,
130, 145–148, 153; relationship
with Adams, 151
Signal Corps, 28, 84
signatures, left-handed, 100
Simson, Bob, 180
Sixth Floor Museum, *134–137*;
Adams and, 149–152; appeal